閱讀測驗答題祕訣

閱讀測驗答題祕訣① —— 尋找關鍵字

1. 整篇文章中，最重要就是第一句和最後一句，第一句稱爲主題句，最後一句稱爲結尾句。每段的第一句和最後一句，第二重要，是該段落的主題句和結尾句。

2. 從「主題句」和「結尾句」中，找出相同的關鍵字，就是文章的重點。因爲美國人從小被訓練，寫作文要注重主題句，他們給學生一個題目後，要求主題句和結尾句都必須有關鍵字。

閱讀測驗祕訣② —— 先看題目、畫線、找出答案、標號

考試的時候，先把閱讀測驗題目瀏覽一遍，在文章中掃瞄和題幹中相同的關鍵字，把和題目相關的句子，用線畫起來，便可一目了然。通常一句話只會考一題，你畫了線以後，再標上題號，接下來，你找其他題目的答案，就會更快了。以104年指定科目考試的試題爲例：

104 學年度指定科目考試英文試題

The first Fabergé egg was crafted for Tsar Alexander III, who gave his wife, the Empress Maria Fedorovna, an Easter egg to celebrate their 20th wedding anniversary. He placed an order with a young jeweler, *Peter Carl Fabergé*, whose beautiful creations had *caught Maria's eye* earlier. On Easter morning of 1885, what appeared to be a simple enameled egg was delivered to the palace. But to the delight of the Empress, the egg opened to a golden yolk; within the yolk was a golden hen; and concealed within the hen was *a diamond* miniature of the royal *crown and a tiny ruby egg*. Unfortunately, the last two surprises are now *lost* to history.

36. Why did Tsar Alexander III choose *Peter Fabergé* to make *the first Easter egg*?
     (A) Peter Fabergé was the goldsmith for the royal family.
     (B) ***Empress Maria was impressed by Peter Fabergé's work***.
     (C) Tsar Alexander III received an order from Empress Maria.
     (D) Peter Fabergé owned the most famous Russian jewelry house.

37. What went *missing* from the first Fabergé egg?
     (A) A golden hen and a ruby egg.
     (B) A golden hen and a golden yolk.
     (C) ***A ruby egg and a diamond crown***.
     (D) A golden yolk and a diamond crown.

　　這兩題的關鍵句就在第一句和最後一句，分別是36題和37題的題幹，斜黑字體就是關鍵字，專有名詞很好找，像是 *Peter Fabergé*，馬上就可以找到對應的上下文，「定位」出答案的句子，但是通常答案會換句話說，這時候要找同義字，36 題的文章關鍵字是 *caught Maria's eye*，換個同義說法，就是 Empress *Maria was impressed*。而 37 題的文章關鍵字是 *lost*，同義字是 *missing*，往上面找就可以馬上找到 a diamond crown 和 a ruby egg。

　　「全真閱讀測驗詳解」囊括近兩年大陸、日本大學入學試題，題材多元，舉凡人文、科學、醫學、哲學，以及跨文化的題材皆納入其中。除了可以練習閱讀，還能增廣見聞，作為一般閱讀的材料。文中所有的內容，都有詳細說明，一目了然。

　　本書雖經謹慎校對，仍恐有疏漏之處，誠盼各界先進不吝指正。

編者　謹識

Test 1
（2014 年大陸山東卷）

One morning, Ann's neighbor Tracy found a lost dog wandering around the local elementary school. She asked Ann if she could keep an eye on the dog. Ann said that she could watch it only for the day.

Tracy took photos of the dog and printed off 400 FOUND fliers（傳單）, and put them in mailboxes. Meanwhile, Ann went to the dollar store and bought some pet supplies, warning her two sons not to fall in love with the dog. At the time, Ann's son Thomas was 10 years old, and Jack, who was recovering from a heart operation, was 21 years old.

Four days later Ann was still looking after the dog, whom they had started to call Riley. When she arrived home from work, the dog threw itself against the screen door and barked madly at her. As soon as she opened the door, Riley dashed into the boys' room, where Ann found Jack suffering a heart attack. Riley ran over to Jack, but as soon as Ann bent over to help him, the dog went silent.

"If it hadn't come to get me, the doctor said Jack would have died," Ann reported to a local newspaper. At this point, no one had called to claim the dog, so Ann decided to keep it.

The next morning Tracy got a call. A man named Peter had recognized his lost dog and called the number on the flier. Tracy started crying, and told him, "That dog saved my friend's son."

Peter drove to Ann's house to pick up his dog, and saw Thomas and Jack crying in the window. After a few moments Peter said, "Maybe Odie was supposed to find you; maybe you should keep him."

【2014 年大陸山東卷】

( ) 1. What did Tracy do after finding the dog?
   A. She looked for its owner.
   B. She gave it to Ann as a gift.
   C. She sold it to the dollar store.
   D. She bought some food for it.

(　) 2. How did the dog help save Jack?

　　　A. By breaking the door for Ann.

　　　B. By leading Ann to Jack's room.

　　　C. By dragging Jack out of the room.

　　　D. By attending Jack when Ann was out.

(　) 3. What was Ann's attitude to the in Paragraph 4?

　　　A. Sympathetic.　　B. Doubtful.

　　　C. Tolerant.　　　D. Grateful.

(　) 4. For what purpose did Peter call Tracy?

　　　A. To help her friend's son.

　　　B. To interview Tracy.

　　　C. To take back his dog.

　　　D. To return the flier to her.

(　) 5. What can we infer about the dog from the last paragraph?

　　　A. It will be given to Odie.

　　　B. It will be kept by Ann's family.

　　　C. It will be returned to Peter.

　　　D. It will be taken away by Tracy.

Test 1 詳解

（2014 年大陸山東卷）

【第一段】

One morning, Ann's neighbor Tracy found a lost dog

wandering around the local elementary school. She asked Ann

[*if* she could keep an eye on the dog]. Ann said [*that* she could
　名詞子句　　　　　　　　　　　　　　　　　　　　　名詞子句

watch it *only for the day.*]

　　有一天早晨，安的鄰居崔西發現一隻迷路的狗，在當地小學附近遊蕩。她問安是否能夠看著這隻狗。安說她只能照顧它一天。

keep an eye on 照料（= *look after*）
for the day 當天（= *for today*）　　***during the day*** 在白天

【第二段】

Tracy took photos *of the dog **and*** printed off 400 FOUND

fliers（傳單）, ***and*** put them *in mailboxes.*

　　崔西替狗拍照，印出 400 張尋找狗主人啟事，把傳單塞在信箱裡。

take photos of 替～拍照
*= **take pictures of***

主人尋找狗，用 "LOST"。

撿到狗尋找主人，用 "FOUND"。

Meanwhile, Ann went to the dollar store *and* bought some pet supplies, *warning her two sons not to fall in love with the dog.*
同時，安去了一元商店，買了一些寵物用品，警告她二個兒子不要愛上這隻狗。

> warning her.... 是分詞構句，相當於 and warned her....，表示對前面的話進一步說明，也表示同時的動作。
>
> *dollar store*　一元商店【廉價商店，不一定全部一元】

At the time, Ann's son Thomas was 10 years old, *and* Jack,
　　　　　　　　　　　　　　　　　　　　　　　　　　　　主詞
who was recovering from a heart operation, was 21 years old.
　　　　　　　　　　　　　　　　　　　　　　　　　　　　動詞
那時，安的兒子湯瑪士 10 歲，而傑克 21 歲，他動完心臟手術正逐漸恢復。

> *at the time*　那時
> *= at that time*

【第三段】

Four days later Ann was *still* looking after the dog,
whom they had started to call Riley.
四天後，安仍然在照顧那隻狗，他們開始叫牠萊利。

> 寫文章常用同義字，到目前爲止已經用了 *keep an eye on*，*watch*，和 *look after*，三個都指「照顧」，背同義字有助於寫作。

When *she arrived home from work*, the dog threw itself against

the screen door ***and*** barked *madly* at her.

當她下班回到家時，狗猛撲過去撞到紗門，對著她狂吠。

> ***throw*** *oneself* ***against*** 撲過去撞到【字典上有 ***throw*** *oneself* ***at***
> 「向~猛撲過去」】
> = ***run into***
> ***screen door*** 紗門

As soon as *she opened the door*, Riley dashed into the boys'

room, ***where*** *Ann found Jack suffering a heart attack*.

她一開門，萊利就衝進男孩的房間，在房裡，安發現傑克心臟病發作。

> ***dash into*** 衝進 (= *rush into*)
>
> 在 where 子句中，suffering... 是分詞片語，做受詞補
> 語，補充說明 Jack。原題中，where 前面無逗點，應改
> 成 ...room, where...，因為 where 引導的形容詞子句是
> 補述用法，要加逗點。【詳見「文法寶典」p.161, p.162】

Riley ran over to Jack, but ***as soon as*** *Ann bent over to help*

him, the dog went silent.

萊利（狗）跑過去傑克身邊，但是當安彎下來幫他時，狗就不叫了。

> ***run over to*** 跑過去　　***go silent*** 變安靜
> = ***rush over to***　　= ***become silent***

【第四段】

*"**If** it hadn't come to get me*, the doctor said [Jack would
　　　　　　　　　　　　　　　　　　　　　　　—名詞子句

have died]," Ann reported *to a local newspaper*.
安向當地的報社說：「如果狗沒有來叫我，醫生說傑克就死了。」

> the doctor said 不是假設法，是插入語，if 子句和 Jack
> would have died 都是與過去事實相反的假設法。
> report 主要意思是「報告」，這裡作「說；敘述」解。

At this point, no one had called *to claim the dog*, *so* Ann
decided <u>to keep it</u>.
　　　　　名詞片語
在此時，沒有人打電話來認領這隻狗，所以安決定把牠留下。

> to claim the dog 不定詞片語修飾 called，表「目的」，
> 不定詞片語 to keep it 做 decided 的受詞。

> *at this point* 在此時【point 時刻】
> = *at the time*【前面已用】
> claim *v.* 認領；宣稱

【第五段】

The next morning Tracy got a call.　A man *named Peter*

had recognized his lost dog *and* called the number *on the flier*.
Tracy started crying, *and* told him, "That dog saved my
friend's son."

　　隔天早上，崔西接到一通電話。一個名叫彼德的人認出他遺失的狗，打了傳單上的電話。崔西開始哭，告訴他：「那隻狗救了我朋友的兒子。」

　　動名詞 crying 做 started 的受詞，也可用 to cry。【詳見「文法寶典」p.434】

【第六段】

Peter drove to Ann's *house to pick up his dog*, **and** saw Thomas and Jack *crying in the window*. ***After a few moments*** Peter said, "Maybe Odie was supposed *to find you*; maybe you should keep him."

　　彼德開車到安的家去接他的狗，看到湯瑪斯和傑克在窗戶裡哭。過了一會兒，彼德說：「也許歐弟註定會找到你們，也許你們應該把它留下來。」

　　因為 Peter 從外面往裡面看，所以用 Thomas and Juck crying in the window。

　　be supposed to 主要意思是「應該」，在此指「註定」（ = be destined to ）。

　　在 Maybe Odie…；maybe you… 句中，二個句子之間原來應用 and 連接，在口語中用逗點取代 and。

1.（**A**）發現狗後崔西做了什麼？

　　A. 她尋找狗主人。

　　B. 她把狗送給安當做禮物。

　　C. 她把狗賣給一元商店。

　　D. 她買了一些食物給牠。【不是崔西買的，是安買的】

2.（**B**）這隻狗如何幫助解救傑克？

　　A. 為安把門打破。

　　B. 帶安去傑克的房間。

　　C. 把傑克拖出房間。

　　D. 安不在時照顧傑克。

3.（**D**）根據第四段，安對這隻狗的態度為何？

　　A. 同情的。　　　　　　　B. 懷疑的。

　　C. 容忍的。　　　　　　　D. 感激的。

4.（**C**）彼德為了什麼目的打電話給崔西？

　　A. 為了幫助她朋友的兒子。

　　B. 為了採訪崔西。

　　C. 為了帶回他的狗。

　　D. 為了把傳單還給她。

5.（**B**）從最後一段我們可以推論這隻狗

　　A. 將被送給歐弟。

　　B. 將被安的家人留下來。

　　C. 將被還給彼德。

　　D. 將被崔西帶走。

Test 2
(2014 年大陸全國新課標卷)

Passenger pigeons（旅鴿）*once* flew over much of the United States in unbelievable numbers. Written accounts from the 18th and 19th centuries described flocks（群）so large that they darkened the sky for hours.

It was calculated that when the population reached its highest point, there were more than 3 billion passenger pigeons—a number equal to 24 to 40 percent of the total bird population in the United States, making it perhaps the most abundant bird in the world. Even as late as 1870, when their numbers had already become smaller, a flock believed to be 1 mile wide and 320 miles (about 515 kilometers) long was seen near Cincinnati.

Sadly, the abundance of passenger pigeons may have been their <u>undoing</u>. Where the birds were most abundant, people believed there was an ever-lasting supply and killed them by the thousands. Commercial hunters attracted them to small clearings with grain, waited until pigeons had settled to feed, and threw large nets over them, taking hundreds at a time. The birds were shipped to large cities and sold in restaurants.

By the closing decades of the 19th century, the hardwood forests where passenger pigeons nested had been damaged by Americans' need for wood, which scattered (驅散) the flocks and forced the birds to go farther north, where cold temperatures and spring storms contributed to their decline. Soon the great flocks were gone, never to be seen again.

In 1897, the state of Michigan passed a law prohibiting the killing of passenger pigeons, but by then, no sizable flocks had been seen in the state for 10 years. The last confirmed wild pigeon in the United States was shot by a boy in Pike County, Ohio, in 1900. For a time, a few birds survived under human care. The last of them, known affectionately as Martha, died at the Cincinnati Zoological Garden on September 1, 1914. 【2014 年大陸全國新課標卷】

(   ) 1. In the 18th and early 19th centuries, passenger pigeons _____.

A. were the biggest bird in the world

B. lived mainly in the south of America

C. did great harm to the national environment

D. were the largest bird population in the US

(   ) 2. The underlined word "undoing" probably refers to the pigeons' _____.

A. escape   B. ruin

C. liberation   D. evolution

(   ) 3. What was the main reason for people to kill passenger pigeons?

A. To seek pleasure.   B. To save other birds.

C. To make money.   D. To protect crops.

(   ) 4. What can we infer about the law passed in Michigan?

A. It was ignored by the public.

B. It was declared too late.

C. It was unfair.

D. It was strict.

Test 2　詳解
（2014 年大陸全國新課標卷）

【第一段】

Passenger pigeons *once* flew *over much of the United States*

in unbelievable number.

　　旅鴿曾經以令人難以置信的數目，飛過美國許多地區的上空。

> ***passenger pigeon*** 旅鴿【又稱「野鴿」（= *wild pigeon*）】
>
> 　【旅鴿，又名候鴿、旅行鴿，曾經是世界上最常見的一種鳥類。主要以植物果實和小昆蟲為食。據估計，過去曾有多達 50 億隻的旅鴿生活在美國】
>
> 　【比較】***messenger pigeon*** 信鴿

passenger pigeon

Written accounts *from the 18th and 19th centuries* described

flocks *so* large ***that* they darkened the sky for hours.**

十八和十九世紀的書面記錄，描述成群的旅鴿是如此地龐大，以致於遮住天空好幾個小時。

> account〔əˈkaʊnt〕*n.* 報告　　flock〔flɑk〕*n.*（鳥、羊）群

【第二段】

It was calculated ***that when* the population reached its** *highest point*, there were more than 3 billion passenger

pigeons—…

　　據估計，當旅鴿的數量達到最高峰時，有三十億隻旅鴿——…

　　population 主要的意思是「人口數」，在此指「（生物）群

體數」。

> *It is calculated that*… 據估計…
> *It is reported that*… 據報導…
> *It is said that*… 據說…
> *It is agreed that*… 大家都同意…

【詳見「文法寶典」p.377】

…— a number (*which was*) *equal to 24 to 40 percent of the*

total bird population in the United States, making it perhaps

the most abundant bird in the world.

…——這個數字等於美國鳥類總數的百分之二十四至四十，使牠可能

成爲全世界數量最多的鳥類。

　　破折號（——）表示對前面加以説明。

　　equal to 源自 which was equal to。

　　abundant〔ə'bʌndənt〕的主要意思是「豐富的」，在此指

「大量的」。

背這個字，要三個字一起背：underline{abound} *v.* 充滿，underline{abundant}
adj. 豐富的，underline{abundance} *n.* 豐富。【詳見「一口氣背7000字」p.1】
perhaps（或許）是副詞，修飾後面的名詞片語，類似用
法的副詞有：only, not, even 等。【詳見「文法寶典」p.263】

Even as late *as 1870,* **when** *their numbers had already become*

smaller, a flock | *believed to be 1 mile wide **and** 320 miles*

(about 515 kilometers) long | was seen *near Cincinnati.*

甚至晚至 1870 年，這時牠們的數量已經變少了，被認為有一英里寬，
320 英里（大約 515 公里）長的一群旅鴿，在辛辛那提的附近被看見。

believe 主要作「相信」解，這裡是「認為」。

Cincinnati〔͵sɪnsəˈnætɪ〕*n.* 辛辛那提【美國俄亥俄州（Ohio）
　　西南部的一個城市】

【第三段】

Sadly, the abundance *of passenger pigeons* may have been
their underline{undoing}.

令人遺憾的是，旅鴿的數量龐大，可能就是牠們毀滅的原因。

sad〔ˈsædlɪ〕*adv.* 不幸地；遺憾地（= *unfortunately*）
undoing〔ʌnˈduɪŋ〕*n.* 毀滅；毀滅的原因

Where the birds were most abundant, people believed *there*

*was an ever-lasting supply **and** killed them by the thousands.*

在這些鳥最多的地方，人們認爲牠們會源源不絕出現，所以就殺了數
以千計的鳥。

> Where 是表地點的從屬連接詞，作「在…的地方」解 (= *in
> the places where*)。where 也可放在句首。【詳見「文法寶
> 典」p.498】
>
> everlasting 〔ˌɛvəˈlæstɪŋ〕 *adj.* 永久的；無窮盡的
>
> supply 的主要是當動詞，作「供給」解，在此是名詞，作
> 「供應；補給；供給量」解。
>
> *by the thousands* 以千計
>
> 「by + the + 名詞」表「以～計」。【詳見「文法寶典」p.566】

Commercial hunters attracted them *to small clearings*

with grain, ...

以營利爲目的的獵人，會用穀物把牠們吸引到小的林中空地，…

> commercial 〔kəˈmɝʃəl〕 *adj.* 商業的；營利的；以獲利爲目的的
> clearing 〔ˈklɪrɪŋ〕 *n.* (林中的) 空地

…, waited ***until** pigeons had settled to feed*, and threw large

nets *over them*, taking hundreds *at a time*.

…，等到這些鴿子停下來吃東西，就把大張的網子撒在他們身上，一次就抓好幾百隻。

> settle〔ˈsɛt!〕*v.* 棲息；停下來
>
> ***at a time***　一次（= *at once*）
>
> then 是 and then 的省略，連接三個動詞：attracted, waited 和 threw，表三個連續的動作。有時爲了表示緊湊、一氣呵成，會將 and 省略。【詳見「文法寶典」p.465】
> 類似的有：Work hard, study hard, play hard. (= *Work hard, study hard, and play hard.*)

The birds were shipped *to large cities **and** sold in restaurants.*
這些鳥被運送到大城市，並且在餐廳出售。

> ship 的主要意思是「船」，在這裡是動詞，作「運送」解。

【第四段】

By the closing decades *of the 19th century*, the hardwood

forests ***where** passenger pigeons nested* had been damaged *by*

Americans' need for wood, …

到了十九世紀最後十年的時候，旅鴿會在那裡築巢的闊葉樹林，因爲美國人需要木材而受到破壞…

closing 〔'klozɪŋ〕*adj.* 即將結束的

hardwood 〔'hɑrd,wud〕*n.* 硬木材【傢俱材料】

hardwood forest 闊葉森林【通常為 hardwood trees 所組成，

如楓樹（maple）、橡樹（oak）等】

… need for wood, ***which*** *scattered the flocks **and** forced the*

birds to go farther north, ***where*** *cold temperatures **and** spring*

storms contributed to their decline.

…，這樣的需求驅散了鳥群，迫使牠們前往北方，那裡寒冷的天氣和春天的暴風雨，使牠們數量減少。

contribute 〔kən'trɪbjut〕的主要意思是「貢獻」，contribute to 有正反兩面的意思：①促成；有助於 ②導致。

decline 〔dɪ'klaɪn〕主要是當動詞，作「衰退；減少」解，在此是名詞，作「（數量）減少」解。

Soon *the great flocks were gone, never to be seen again.*

不久，大群的鳥就消失了，再也看不到了。

soon 〔sun〕*adv.* 不久（= *before long*）

【第五段】

In 1897, the state of Michigan passed a law *prohibiting*

the killing of passenger pigeons, ***but*** by then, no sizable flocks

had been seen *in the state for 10 years*.

在 1897 年，密西根州通過一條法律，禁止獵殺旅鴿，但到了那時候，在密西根州已經有十年沒看到過龐大的鳥群。

sizeable〔ˈsaɪzəbḷ〕*adj.* 相當大的【它的名詞是 size「大小；尺寸」】

The last confirmed wild pigeon *in the United States* was shot

by a boy in Pike County, Ohio, in 1900.

在美國最後一隻經過證實的野鴿，在 1900 年，於俄亥俄州的派克郡，被一名小男孩所射殺。

For a time, a few birds survived *under human care*.

有一段時間，有些鳥在人類的照顧之下還活著。

for a time　有一段時間（＝*for a while*）

The last *of them*, *(which was)* known affectionately as Martha,

died *at the Cincinnati Zoological Garden on September 1, 1914*.

其中的最後一隻，被親切地稱爲瑪莎，1914 年 9 月 1 日，死於辛辛那提動物園。

> ***be known as*** 被稱爲　　Martha〔'mɑrθə〕*n.* 瑪莎
> affectionately〔ə'fɛkʃənıtlı〕*adv.* 充滿深情地；溫柔親切地
> ***zoological garden*** 動物園（= *zoo*）

1.(**D**) 在十八世紀和十九世紀初，旅鴿 ＿＿＿＿＿＿。

　　　A. 是全世界最大的鳥

　　　B. 主要是生活在美國南部

　　　C. 對全國的環境有相當大的傷害

　　　D. 是美國數量最多的鳥

2.(**B**) 劃底線的字 "undoing" 可能是指鴿子的 ＿＿＿＿＿。

　　　A. 逃走　　　　　　　B. 毀滅

　　　C. 解放　　　　　　　D. 進化

3.(**C**) 人們殺死旅鴿的主要原因是什麼？

　　　A. 爲了尋找快樂。　　　B. 爲了救其他的鳥。

　　　C. 爲了賺錢。　　　　　D. 保護農作物。

4.(**B**) 關於在密西根州通過的法律，我們可以推論出什麼？

　　　A. 被大衆所忽視。　　　B. 太晚宣布。

　　　C. 並不公平。　　　　　D. 很嚴格。

Test 3

（2014 年大陸全國新課標卷）

Since the first Earth Day in 1970, Americans have gotten a lot "greener" toward the environment. "We didn't know at that time that there even was an environment, let alone that there was a problem with it," says Bruce Anderson, president of Earth Day USA.

But what began as nothing important in public affairs has grown into a social movement. Business people, political leaders, university professors, and especially millions of grass-roots Americans are taking part in the movement. "The understanding has increased many, many times," says Gaylord Nelson, the former governor from Wisconsin, who thought up the first Earth Day.

According to US government reports, emissions （排放） from cars and trucks have dropped from 10.3 million tons a year to 5.5 million tons. The number of cities producing CO beyond the standard has been reduced from 40 to 9. Although serious problems still remain and need to be dealt with, the world is a safer and healthier place. A kind of "green thinking" has become part of practices.

Great improvement has been achieved. In 1988 there were only 600 recycling programs; today in 1995 there are about 6,600. Advanced lights, motors, and building designs have helped save a lot of energy and therefore prevented pollution.

Twenty-five years ago, there were hardly any education programs for the environment. Today, it's hard to find a public school, university, or law school that does not have such a program. "Until we do that, nothing else will change!" says Bruce Anderson.

【2014 年大陸全國新課標卷】

(　　) 1. According to Anderson, before 1970, Americans had little idea about _____.
   A. the social movement
   B. recycling techniques
   C. environmental problems
   D. the importance of Earth Day

(　) 2. Where does the support for environmental
　　　 protection mainly come from?
　　　 A.　The grass-roots level.
　　　 B.　Business circles.
　　　 C.　Government officials.
　　　 D.　University professors.

(　) 3. What have Americans achieved in
　　　 environmental protection?
　　　 A.　They have cut car emissions to the
　　　　　 lowest.
　　　 B.　They have settled their environmental
　　　　　 problems.
　　　 C.　They have lowered their CO levels in
　　　　　 forty cities.
　　　 D.　They have reduced pollution through
　　　　　 effective measures.

(　) 4. What is especially important for
　　　 environmental protection according to the
　　　 last paragraph?
　　　 A.　Education.　　　 B.　Planning.
　　　 C.　Green living.　　 D.　CO reduction.

Test 3 詳解

（2014 年大陸全國新課標卷）

【第一段】

Since the first Earth Day in 1970, Americans have gotten

a lot "greener" *toward the environment.*

自從 1970 年第一個世界地球日，美國人已經對環境變得「更綠」
許多。

greener 字面的意思是「更綠的」，在此指「更環保的」。

Earth Day 世界地球日【每年4月22日是全世界環保主義者的節日】

"We didn't know *at that time **that** there even was an environment,*

*let alone **that** there was a problem with it,*" says Bruce Anderson,

president *of Earth Day USA.*

「我們那時候甚至不知道有「環境」這個東西，更不用說環境有什麼
問題了，」美國世界地球日會長布魯斯・安德森說。

at that time 當時（= then）

下面是獨立不定片語，和其他部份的文法無關而獨立存在。

$$\begin{cases} \textit{\textbf{let alone}} \ \ 更不用說 \\ = \textit{\textbf{to say nothing of}} \\ = \textit{\textbf{not to speak of}} \\ = \textit{\textbf{not to mention}} \end{cases}$$ 【詳見「文法寶典」p.417】

president〔ˈprɛzədənt〕通常作「總統；總裁；主席」解，在此指「會長」，指職稱、身份時，不加冠詞。

【第二段】

But [***what*** *began as nothing important in public affairs*]
—名詞子句

has grown into a *social* movement.

但是，一開始是公共事務中不重要的事情，已經變成了一個社會運動。

what 引導名詞子句，what = the thing that。

grow into 字面的意思是「成長成」，即「變成」(= become)。

social movement 社會運動

Business people, political leaders, university professors, ***and***
名詞片語　　　　名詞片語　　　　名詞片語

especially millions of grass-roots Americans are taking part in
名詞片語　　　　　　　動詞片語

the movement.
受詞

商業人士、政治領袖、大學教授，特別是好幾百萬個基層美國民眾，正在參與這項運動。

grass-roots 字面的意思是「草根」，引申為「一般民眾的」，在這裡做形容詞用，引申為「基層的；一般民眾的」。

take part in 參與 (= participate in = join)

"The understanding has increased *many, many times,"* says

Gaylord Nelson, <u>*the former governor from Wisconsin*</u>, **who**
　　　　　　　　　　　　　　　　　　　　同　位　語

thought up the first Earth Day.

「這樣的共鳴已經成長了很多很多，很多倍，」前威斯康辛州州長蓋
洛德・尼爾森說，他是第一個想出「世界地球日」的人。

> understanding 主要是作「了解；理解」解，這裡是指「共鳴；
> 同感」（= *agreement*）。

> Gaylord Nelson〔'gelɔrd'nɛlsən〕*n.* 蓋洛德・尼爾森
> Wisconsin〔wɪs'kɑnsṇ〕*n.* 威斯康辛州
> **think up** 想出（= *come up with*）

【第三段】

According to US government reports, emissions *from cars*

and *trucks* have dropped *from 10.3 million tons a year to 5.5*

million tons.

　根據美國政府的報告，汽車和卡車的排放物，從一年 1,030 萬噸，
降低到 550 萬噸。

> emission〔ɪ'mɪʃən〕的主要意思是「發射」，在這裡作「放
> 射物」解（= *discharge*），通常用複數形式。

The number *of cities producing CO beyond the standard* has been reduced *from 40 to 9.*

產出一氧化碳超出標準的城市，數量已經從 40 個降到 9 個。

CO *n.* 一氧化碳（= *carbon monoxide*〔məˈnɑksaɪd〕）
producing 源自 which produce。

[*Although* serious problems still remain *and* need to be dealt with], the world is a safer *and* healthier place.

雖然嚴重的問題依然存在，而且需要被處理，全世界是個更安全而且更健康的地方。

remain 是完全不及物動詞，在此作「存在」解。

deal with 處理【deal 的三態變化：deal–dealt–dealt】

A kind *of "green thinking"* has become part *of practices.*

一種「綠色思考」已經變成慣例的一部份。

practice 的主要意思是「練習」，在此作「習慣；慣例」解。

【第四段】

Great improvement has been achieved.
已經獲得很大的進步。

achieve〔əˈtʃiv〕的主要意思是「達成；獲得」，***achieve improvement*** 表示「有進步」。

In 1988 there were *only* 600 recycling programs; today *in 1995* there are about 6,600.
在 1988 年，只有 600 個資源回收方案；現在，在 1995 年，有大約 6,600 個。

today 是轉承語，指「現在」（= *now*）。
recycling〔riˈsaɪklɪŋ〕*n.* 資源回收
program〔ˈprogræm〕的主要意思是「節目；課程」，在此作「計劃；方案」解。

Advanced lights, motors, ***and*** building designs have helped save a lot of energy ***and*** *therefore* prevented pollution.
先進的電燈、馬達和建築設計，已經幫助節省了很多能源，也因此避免了污染。

help (to) + 原形 V.，to 常省略。

【第五段】

Twenty-five years ago, there were *hardly* any education programs *for the environment*.

二十五年前，幾乎沒有任何環境的教育課程。

Today, it's hard *to find a public school*, *university*, *or law school* **that** *does not have such a program*.

現在，很難找到一所公立學校、大學或法學院，沒有這樣的課程。

"*Until we do that*, nothing else will change!" says Bruce Anderson.

「直到我們做了那件事，其他事情才會改變！」布魯斯・安德森說。

not…until「直到～才…」，not 在 nothing 裡面。

1. (**C**) 根據安德森的說法，在 1970 年之前，美國人幾乎不知道

　　　　　　　　 _____。

　　　　A. 社會運動。

　　　　B. 資源回收技巧。

　　　　C. 環境問題。

　　　　D. 世界地球日的重要性。

2. (**A**) 環境保護的支持主要來自哪裡？
    A. 基層民眾。
    B. 商業圈。
    C. 政府官員。
    D. 大學教授。

3. (**D**) 美國人在環境保護這方面達成了什麼？
    A. 他們已經把汽車排放量減到最低。
    B. 他們已經解決了環境問題。
    C. 他們已經降低在 40 個城市裡的一氧化碳含量。
    D. 他們已經透過有效的措施降低污染。

    cut〔kʌt〕v. 減少　　settle〔'sɛtl̩〕v. 解決
    levels〔'lɛvl̩z〕n. pl. 濃度；含量
    measures〔'mɛʒəz〕n. pl. 方法；措施

4. (**A**) 根據最後一段，對環境保護來說，什麼是尤其重要的？
    A. 教育。
    B. 計畫。
    C. 環保的生活方式。
    D. 一氧化碳的減少。

    living〔'lɪvɪŋ〕n. 生活方式（= lifestyle = way of life）

Test 4

（2014 年大陸山東卷）

Elizabeth Freeman was born about 1742 to African American parents who were slaves. At the age of six months she was acquired, along with her sister, by John Ashley, a wealthy Massachusetts slaveholder. She became known as "Mumbet" or "Mum Bett."

For nearly 30 years Mumbet served the Ashley family. One day, Ashley's wife tried to strike Mumbet's sister with a spade. Mumbet protected her sister and took the blow instead. Furious, she left the house and refused to come back. When the Ashleys tried to make her return, Mumbet consulted a lawyer, Theodore Sedgwick. With his help, Mumbet sued（起訴）for her freedom.

While serving the Ashleys, Mumbet had listened to many discussions of the new Massachusetts constitution. If the constitution said that all people were free and equal, then she thought it should apply to her. Eventually, Mumbet won her freedom—the first slave in Massachusetts to do so under the new constitution.

Strangely enough, after the trial, the Ashleys asked Mumbet to come back and work for them as a paid employee. She declined and instead went to work for Sedgwick. Mumbet died in 1829, but her legacy lived on in her many descendants（後裔）. One of her great-grandchildren was W. E. B. Du Bois, one of the founders of the NAACP, and an important writer and spokesperson for African American civil rights.

Mumbet's tombstone still stands in the Massachusetts cemetery where she was buried. It reads, in part: "She was born a slave and remained a slave for nearly thirty years. She could neither read nor write, yet in her own sphere she had no superior or equal."【2014 年 大陸山東卷】

( ) 1. What do we know about Mumbet according to Paragraph 1?
   A. She was born a slave.
   B. She was a slaveholder.
   C. She had a famous sister.
   D. She was born into a rich family.

(　) 2. Why did Mumbet run away from the Ashleys?

    A. She found an employer.

    B. She wanted to be a lawyer.

    C. She was hit and got angry.

    D. She had to take care of her sister.

(　) 3. What did Mumbet learn from discussions about the new constitution?

    A. She should always obey her owners' orders.

    B. She should be as free and equal as whites.

    C. How to be a good servant.

    D. How to apply for a job.

(　) 4. What did Mumbet do after the trial?

    A. She chose to work for a lawyer.

    B. She founded the NAACP.

    C. She continued to serve the Ashleys.

    D. She went to live with her grandchildren.

(　) 5. What is the text mainly about?

    A. A story of a famous writer and spokesperson.

    B. The friendship between a lawyer and a slave.

    C. The life of a brave African American woman.

    D. A trial that shocked the whole world.

Test 4 詳解

（2014 年大陸山東卷）

【第一段】

Elizabeth Freeman **was born** about 1742 **to** African

American parents **who** were slaves.

伊麗莎白·費里曼大約出生於 1742 年，父母親是非裔美國人，他們是奴隸。

be born to ①出生於　②由…所生

Elizabeth Freeman〔ɪˈlɪzəbəθ ˈfrimən〕*n.* 伊麗莎白·費里曼

At the age of six months she was acquired, *along with her sister,*

by John Ashley, a wealthy Massachusetts slaveholder.
　　　　　　　　　　同位語

在她六個月大時，她和她姐姐一起被約翰·艾胥黎買走，他是一個富有的麻州蓄奴者。

acquire 的主要意思是「獲得」，在此作「買」（ = *buy* = *purchase* ）解。

along with 連同；和（ = *together with* ）

Ashley〔ˈæʃlɪ〕*n.* 艾胥黎

Massachusetts〔ˌmæsəˈtʃusɛts〕*n.* 麻薩諸塞州

slaveholder〔ˈslevˌholdɚ〕*n.* 奴隸擁有者

【比較】stockholder〔ˈstɑkˌholdɚ〕*n.* 股票持有人；股東

She became known as "Mumbet" or "Mum Bett."
她後來被稱爲「孟貝」或「孟‧貝特」。

> ***be known as*** 被稱爲　　***become known as*** 後來被稱爲
> Mumbet〔ˋmʌmˏbɛt〕*n.* 孟貝（= *Mum Bett*）【專有名詞發音字典
> 上無此字】

【第二段】

For nearly 30 years Mumbet served the Ashley family.
孟貝侍奉艾胥黎一家人將近三十年。

> ***the Ashley family*** 艾胥黎一家人（= *the Ashleys*）

One day, Ashley's wife tried to strike Mumbet's sister *with a spade*.
有一天，艾胥黎的妻子，想要用鏟子打孟貝的姐姐。

> spade〔sped〕*n.* 鏟子

spade

Mumbet protected her sister ***and*** took the blow *instead*.
孟貝保護她姐姐，替她挨打。

> blow 的主要意思是「吹」，在此是名詞，作「打；打擊」
> （= *hit* = *stroke*）解。
> ***take the blow*** 挨打（= *take the hit*）
> instead〔ɪnˋstɛd〕*adv.* 代替；頂替；取而代之

Furious, she left the house *and* refused to come back.

她因憤怒而離開家，且拒絕回去。

= *As she was furious*, she left….

= *Being furious*, she left….

When the Ashleys tried to make her return, Mumbet consulted a lawyer, *Theodore Sedgwick*.

當艾胥黎這家人想叫她回去時，孟貝就請教了一位律師西奧多爾・塞吉威克。

> Theodore Sedgwick (ˈθiəˌdɔr ˈsɛdʒwɪk) *n.* 西奧多爾・塞吉威克
>
> 【原文是 Sedgewick，應改成 Sedgwick。】

With his help, Mumbet sued for her freedom.

有他的幫助，孟貝提出訴訟，要求自由。

> *sue sb. for* sth.「控告某人某事；為了…向某人提出告訴」，
> *sb.* 可省略。

【第三段】

While (*she was*) *serving the Ashleys*, Mumbet had listened to many discussions *of the new Massachusetts constitution*.

當服侍艾胥黎一家人時，孟貝已經聽過很多關於新的麻州憲法的討論。

If the constitution said ***that*** all people were free ***and*** equal,
　　　　　　　　　　　　　　　　名　詞　子　句

then she thought it should apply to her.

如果憲法說所有人都是自由和平等的，那麼她認為這個憲法應該適用於她。

　　apply to　適用於
　　【比較】**apply for**　申請

Eventually, Mumbet won her freedom—*the first slave in*

Massachusetts to do so under the new constitution.

最後，孟貝贏得了自由──她是根據麻州新的憲法，第一個獲得自由的奴隸。

　　eventually　*adv.* 最後，是文章中的轉承語，可用 finally 和 in the end 來取代。
　　under 的主要意思是「在…之下」，在此作「依照；根據」（= *according to*）解。

【第四段】

　　Strangely enough, *after the trial*, the Ashleys asked

Mumbet to come *back **and** work for them as a paid employee.*

奇怪的是，在審判後，艾胥黎一家人要求孟貝回去，並且以受薪雇員的身份為他們工作。

> ***strangely enough*** 奇怪的是；說來奇怪 (= *oddly enough* = *curiously enough*) 這個副詞片語可當轉承語來看，連接前面的句子。

She declined ***and*** *instead* went *to work for Sedgwick*.

她婉拒了，反而去替塞吉威克工作。

> 【比較】 decline〔dɪˈklaɪn〕v. (委婉地) 拒絕
>
> refuse〔rɪˈfjuz〕v. (明確地) 拒絕
>
> reject〔rɪˈdʒɛkt〕v. (斷然) 拒絕【最不客氣】

Mumbet died *in 1829*, ***but*** her legacy lived on *in her many descendants*.

孟貝死於 1829 年，但他的遺風繼續存活在她的許多子孫中。

> legacy〔ˈlɛgəsɪ〕的主要意思是「遺產」，在此作「遺留下來的習氣；遺風」解。
>
> ***live on*** 繼續存在 (= *last*)
>
> descendant〔dɪˈsɛndənt〕n. 子孫【descend〔dɪˈsɛnd〕v. 下降；字尾 ant 指「人」】

One *of her great-grandchildren* was W. E. B. Du Bois, one *of*

the founders of the NAACP, and an important writer *and*

spokesperson *for African American civil rights*.

她其中的一位曾孫，是 W. E. B. 杜波依斯，他是全國有色人種協進會
的創立者之一，也是一位重要的作家，和美國黑人民權運動的發言人。

grand-grandchildren　*n.* 曾孫

W. E. B. Du Bois〔du'bɔɪs〕*n.* W. E. B. 杜波依斯（1868-1963）

NAACP　*n.* 全國有色人種協進會（ = *National Association for
the Advancement of Colored People*）

civil rights　（公）民權

【第五段】

Mumbet's tombstone *still* stands *in the Massachusetts*

cemetery ***where*** *she was buried.*

孟貝的墓碑，依然佇立在她被埋葬的麻省公墓。

tombstone〔'tum,ston〕*n.* 墓碑【b 不發音】

stand〔stænd〕*v.* 位於（ = *be located* = *sit*）。

cemetery〔'sɛmə,tɛrɪ〕*n.* 公墓

【比較】graveyard〔'grev,jɑrd〕*n.* 墓地【屬於教堂】

It reads, *in part*: "She was born a slave *and* remained a slave

for nearly thirty years.

墓碑上一部份的文字寫著:「她一出生就是奴隸,而且當奴隸將近三十年。

read 的主要意思是「閱讀」,在此作「寫著」解。

「be born + 補語」指「生來就是」。

in part 一部份

She could *neither* read *nor* write, *yet in her own sphere* she

had no superior *or* equal."

她既不會讀書也不會寫字,但在她自己的領域中,她無人能敵。」

sphere〔sfɪr〕的主要意思是「球體」,在此作「範圍;領域」(=*field*) 解。

superior 主要是當形容詞,作「較優秀的」解,在此是名詞,指「較優秀的人;高手」。

She had no superior or equal. 字面的意思是「她沒有比她優秀的人或和她相匹敵的人。」也就是「她是最棒的;她無人能敵」。美國人常說:You have no equal. (妳無人能比。)(=*You are the best.*)。

1.（**A**）根據第一段，我們可以知道關於孟貝的什麼事？

    A. 她一出生就是奴隸。   B. 她是蓄奴者。

    C. 她有一位有名的姐姐。   D. 她生於富有的家庭。

2.（**C**）為何孟貝會逃離艾胥黎一家人？

    A. 她找到雇主。   B. 她想要當律師。

    C. 她被毆打，很生氣。   D. 她必須照顧她姐姐。

3.（**B**）從關於新憲法的討論中，孟貝得知什麼？

    A. 她應該永遠遵守她主人的命令。

    B. 她應該跟白人一樣自由而平等。

    C. 如何當一位好僕人。

    D. 如何應徵工作。

    white〔hwaɪt〕*n.* 白人　　***apply for*** 應徵

4.（**A**）在審判之後，孟貝做了什麼事？

    A. 她選擇替一位律師工作。

    B. 她創立了全國有色人種協進會。

    C. 她繼續侍奉艾胥黎一家人。

    D. 她想要和她的孫子住在一起。

5.（**C**）本文主要是關於什麼？

    A. 一個有名的作家和發言人的故事。

    B. 律師和奴隸之間的友誼。

    C. 一位勇敢的美國黑人女性的一生。

    D. 一場震驚全世界的審判。

    text〔tɛkst〕*n.* 內文　　shock〔ʃɑk〕*v.* 使震驚

Test 5
（2014 年大陸福建卷）

Perhaps you think you could easily add to your happiness with more money. Strange as it may seem, if you're unsatisfied, the issue is not a lack of means to meet your desires but a lack of desires—not that you cannot satisfy your tastes but that you don't have enough tastes.

Real riches consist of well-developed and hearty capacities（能力）to enjoy life. Most people are already swamped（淹沒）with things. They eat, wear, go and talk too much. <u>They live in too big a house with too many rooms, yet their house of life is a hut.</u>

Your house of life ought to be a mansion（豪宅）, a royal palace. Every new taste, every additional interest, every fresh enthusiasm adds a room. Here are several rooms your house of life should have.

Art should be a desire for you to develop simply because the world is full of beautiful things. If you only understood how to enjoy them and feed your spirit on them, they would make you as happy as finding plenty of ham and eggs when you're hungry.

Literature, classic literature, is a beautiful, richly furnished room where you might find many an hour of rest and refreshment. To gain that love would go toward making you a rich person, for a rich person is not someone who has a library but someone who likes a library.

Music like Mozart's and Bach's shouldn't be absent. Real riches are of the spirit. And when you've brought that spirit up to where classical music feeds it and makes you a little drunk, you have increased your thrills and bettered them. And life is a matter of thrills.

Sports, without which you remain poor, mean a lot in life. No matter who you are, you would be more human, and your house of life would be better supported against the bad days, if you could, and did, play a bit.

Whatever rooms you might add to your house of life, the secret of enjoying life is to keep adding.

【2014 年大陸福建卷】

(　　) 1. The author intends to tell us that _____.

    A. true happiness lies in achieving wealth by fair means

    B. big houses are people's most valued possessions

    C. big houses can in a sense bring richness of life

    D. true happiness comes from spiritual riches

( ) 2. The underlined sentence in the second paragraph implies that _____.

    A. however materially rich, they never seem to be satisfied

    B. however materially rich, they remain spiritually poor

    C. though their house is big, they prefer a simple life

    D. though their house is big, it seems to be a cage

( ) 3. It can be learned from the passage that _____.

    A. more money brings more happiness

    B. art is needed to make your house beautiful

    C. literature can enrich your spiritual life

    D. sports contribute mainly to your physical fitness

( ) 4. What would be the best title for the passage?

    A. House of Life

    B. Secret of Wealth

    C. Rest and Refreshment

    D. Interest and Enthusiasm

Test 5 詳解
（2014 年大陸福建卷）

【第一段】

Perhaps you think you could *easily* add to your happiness
with more money.

或許你認爲，你能輕易地用更多錢增加你的幸福。

這裡用假設法助動詞 could，表示「與現在事實相反」，
因爲作者並不認爲，用更多錢就能增加幸福。

add to 加強；增加（= *increase*）

*Strange **as** it may seem*, **if** *you're unsatisfied*, the issue is **not** <u>a</u>
= Although it may seem strange

<u>lack of means</u> *to meet your desires **but*** <u>a lack of desires</u>—
雖然這看似很奇怪，如果你不滿足，問題不是缺乏錢來滿足你的慾望，
而是缺乏慾望——

as 在第二個字作「雖然」解。【詳見「文法寶典」p.529】
issue 在這裡作「問題」（= *point* = *question*）解。
means 的主要意思是「方法；手段」，在此作「財富；金錢」
（= *money* = *wealth*）解。

not A ***but*** B　不是 A，而是 B【是對等連詞】

$$\left.\begin{array}{l} \textit{meet} \\ \textit{satisfy} \\ \textit{fulfill} \end{array}\right\} \textit{one's desire} \quad 滿足某人的慾望$$

not <u>that</u> you cannot satisfy your tastes ***but*** <u>that</u> you don't have

$\quad\quad$‖$\quad\quad\quad\quad\quad\quad\quad\quad\quad\quad\quad\quad\quad\quad\quad\quad$‖

$\quad$because$\quad\quad\quad\quad\quad\quad\quad\quad\quad\quad\quad\quad\quad$because

enough tastes.

不是因為你無法滿足你的嗜好，而是因為你沒有足夠的嗜好。

> 破折號（—）表示總括全句的意思。【詳見「文法寶典」p.42】
> taste 的主要意思是「味道；品味」，在此作「愛好；嗜好」
> （ = *liking* = *preference* ）解。

【第二段】

Real riches consist of *well-developed* ***and*** *hearty* capacities

to enjoy life.

　　真正的財富，是有發展健全，且旺盛的能力，去享受生活。【也就是「要有品味享受生活」。】

> riches 和 means 作「財富」解時，要用複數形。
> hearty 的主要意思是「衷心的；熱誠的」，在這裡作「旺盛的；強健的」（ = *strong* = *active* ）解。
> riches〔ˈrɪtʃɪz〕*n. pl.* 財富 (= *wealth* = *means*)
> ***consist of*** 由…組成 (= *be made up of* = *be composed of*)
> well-developed〔ˌwɛl dɪˈvɛləpd〕*adj.* 健全的；發展良好的

capacity〔kə'pæsətɪ〕*n.* 能力 (= *power* = *ability*)

Most people are *already* swamped *with things.*
大部份的人已經忙於應付許多事情。

> swamp 的主要意思是「淹沒」，***be swamped with***「被～
> 淹沒；忙於應付」。

They eat, wear, go *and* talk *too much.*
他們吃太多、穿太多、走太多，而且說太多。

They live *in too big a house with too many rooms,* **yet** their
house *of life* is a hut.
他們住的房子太大，有太多房間，但是他們人生的房子卻是個小屋。

> too big a house「一個太大的房子」；倒裝的原因詳見「文
> 法寶典」p.216。
>
> hut〔hʌt〕*n.* (簡陋的) 小屋 (= *a small simple building*)

【第三段】

Your house *of life* ought to be a mansion, a royal palace.
你人生的房子應該是一個豪宅，一個皇宮。

> mansion〔'mænʃən〕*n.* 豪宅 (= *a large and imposing house*)

royal〔'rɔɪəl〕adj. 皇家的　　palace〔'pælɪs〕n. 宮殿

Every new taste, *every* additional interest, *every* fresh

enthusiasm adds a room.

每一個新的嗜好、每一個新增加的興趣，每一個新的熱衷的事物，都添加了一個房間。

　　注意：三個名詞沒有連接詞，省略 and，表示一氣呵成。

　　【詳見「文法寶典」p.649】

　　every 後接單數名詞，雖然多個，也用單數動詞 adds。

additional〔ə'dɪʃənḷ〕adj. 額外的；附加的

fresh〔frɛʃ〕adj. 新鮮的；新的

enthusiasm〔ɪn'θjuzɪ,æzəm〕n. 巨大的興趣；熱忱；熱中的事物

Here are several rooms *your house of life should have.*

這裡有幾個，你人生房子應該有的房間。

【第四段】

　　Art should be a desire *for you to develop simply **because***

the world is full of beautiful things.

　　藝術應該是你可以培養的愛好，完全因為這世界上充滿著美麗的事物。

desire 的主要意思是「慾望；渴望」，在此作「渴望的事物；想要的東西」(＝ *something or someone that is desired*) 解。

simply 主要的意思是「簡單地」，在此作「只是；完全」解。

be full of 充滿著～

[***If*** *you only understood how to enjoy them* ***and*** *feed your spirit on them,*] they would make you *as* happy ***as*** *finding plenty of ham and eggs* ***when*** *you're hungry.*

你只要能了解如何欣賞它們，並且用美麗的事物滋養你的靈魂，它們會讓你感到高興，就和當你飢餓時找到許多火腿蛋一樣。

feed~on *sth.* 用某物餵養～；用某物充實～

ham and eggs

【第五段】

Literature, *classic literature*, is a beautiful, *richly* furnished room ***where*** *you might find many an hour of rest* ***and*** *refreshment.*

文學、經典文學，是個美麗、佈置華麗的房間，在這裡你可以找到好幾個小時的休息和恢復精神。

classic literature (經典文學) 補充說明 literature。

furnish 是「使配置傢俱」，它的名詞是 furniture (傢俱)，

furnished room 是「有傢俱的房間」。

richly〔'rɪtʃlɪ〕*adv.* 華麗地；豐富地

many a + 單數名詞 = many + 複數名詞，表「很多」，語氣較強。

refreshment〔rɪ'frɛʃmənt〕*n.* 恢復精神

複數形 refreshments 則作「點心」(= *snacks*) 解。

<u>To gain that love</u> would go toward making you a rich person,
不定詞片語當名詞用，做主詞

for a rich person is *not someone who* has a library *but someone*

who likes a library.

如果能得到那種喜好，就有助於使你成為富有的人，因為富有的人不是一個擁有圖書館的人，而是喜歡圖書館的人。

To gain that love 是不定詞片語當主詞，含有 if 的意思，因主要子句有假設法助動詞 would。【詳見「文法寶典」p.367】

for 是用來解釋的對等連接詞，作「因為」解。【詳見「文法寶典」p.476】

go toward 有助於 (= *contribute to*)

not A *but* B 不是 A，而是 B

【第六段】

Music *like Mozart's and Bach's* shouldn't be absent.

像莫札特和巴哈的音樂，不應該沒有。

Mozart〔'mozɑrt〕*n.* 莫札特【奧地利作曲家】

Bach〔bɑk〕*n.* 巴哈【德國風琴家及作曲家】

absent〔ˈæbsn̩t〕*adj.* 缺席的;沒有的;不在的

Real riches are of the spirit. 真正的富有是心靈上的。

= Real riches are (*the riches*) of the spirit.

= Real riches come from the spirit.

And *when you've brought that spirit up to **where classical music***

feeds it and makes you a little drunk, you have increased your

名

詞　　　子　　　句

thrills ***and*** bettered them.

而當你已經把那種心靈帶到古典音樂所滋養的地方,並讓你有點陶醉

在其中,你已經增加並提高你的興奮感。

> ***bring…up to*** 字面的意思是「把…往上帶到」,引申為「把…
> 提升到(某標準、程度)」(=*raise…to*)。
>
> drunk〔drʌŋk〕*adj.* 陶醉的　　　thrill〔θrɪl〕*n.* 興奮
> better〔ˈbɛtɚ〕*v.* 改善;提高

And life is a matter of thrills. 而且生命就是攸關興奮的問題。

> a matter of …的問題
>
> a matter of time 時間的問題
>
> a matter of life and death 攸關生死的問題

【第七段】

Sports, *without **which** you remain poor*, mean *a lot in life*.

運動在生命中非常重要，沒有運動，你依然貧窮。

mean a lot 意義重大；很重要

演講時常說：

Ladies and gentlemen,

Being here means a lot to me.（來到這裡對我意義重大。）

No matter** who you are*, you would be *more* human, ***and your

house *of life* would be *better* supported against the bad days,

***if** you could, **and** did, play a bit.*

無論你是誰，你會更有人性，而你人生的房子將會更能夠抵抗壞天氣，
如果你能夠，而且能真的有稍微運動。

bad days 字面上是「不好的日子」，在此指「壞天氣」。

do + 原形動詞，表「真的…」。

play 一作是「遊玩」，在此作「參加體育活動；運動」

（= *take part in a sport*）解。

human〔'hjumən〕*n.* 人類　*adj.* 有人性的

a bit 有點；稍微

【第八段】

Whatever *rooms you might add to your house of life*, the

secret *of enjoying life* is to keep adding.

不管你加了什麼房間到你的人生房子裡，享受人生的祕訣，就是
持續地增加房間。

add A **to** B　把 A 加到 B　　**keep + V-ing** 持續~

1. (**D**) 作者意圖要告訴我們 _____。
    A. 真正的幸福在於用正當的方式獲得財富
    B. 大房子是人們最珍貴的財產
    C. 大房子在某種意義上會帶來生命的富裕
    D. 真正的幸福來自心靈上的財富

    intend to V. 意圖~；打算~
    lie in 在於 (= *consist in*)　　achieve〔əˋtʃiv〕*v.* 獲得
    fair〔fɛr〕*adj.* 公正的；正當的
    means〔minz〕*n. pl.* 方法；手段
    valued〔ˋvæljud〕*adj.* 受重視的；貴重的
    in a sense 在某種意義上

2. (**B**) 在第二段劃底線的句子可能是暗示_____。
    A. 無論物質上多富足，他們似乎永遠無法滿足
    B. 無論物質上多富足，他們心靈上還是貧窮
    C. 雖然他們的房子很大，他們偏好樸實的生活
    D. 雖然他們的房子很大，還是看似一個牢籠

underlined〔ˌʌndɚˈlaɪnd〕*adj.* 劃底線的

materially〔məˈtɪrɪəlɪ〕*adv.* 物質上

cage〔kedʒ〕*n.* 籠子

3. (**C**) 從本文中可以得知 ＿＿＿＿＿＿。

　　A. 更多的錢帶來更多的幸福

　　B. 需要藝術來使你的房子更漂亮

　　C. 文學可以豐富你的精神生活

　　D. 運動主要是有助於你的身體健康

　　　learn〔lɝn〕*v.* 知道

　　　enrich〔ɪnˈrɪtʃ〕*v.* 使豐富

　　　contribute to 有助於

　　　physical〔ˈfɪzɪk!〕*adj.* 身體的

　　　fitness〔ˈfɪtnɪs〕*n.* 健康

4. (**A**) 本文最好的標題是什麼？

　　A. 生命的房子

　　B. 財富的秘訣

　　C. 休息和恢復精神

　　D. 興趣和熱忱

Test 6
（2014 年大陸江蘇卷）

However wealthy we may be, we can never find enough hours in the day to do everything we want. Economics deals with this problem through the concept of opportunity cost, which simply refers to whether someone's time or money could be better spent on something else.

Every hour of our time has a value. For every hour we work at one job we could quite easily be doing another, or be sleeping or watching a film. Each of these options has a different opportunity cost—namely, *what they cost us in missed opportunities.*

Say you intend to watch a football match, but the tickets are expensive and it will take you a couple of hours to get to and from the stadium. Why not, you might reason, watch the game from home and use the <u>leftover</u> money and <u>time</u> to have dinner with friends? This—the alternative use of your cash and time—is the opportunity cost.

For economists, every decision is made by knowledge of what one must forgo—in terms of money and enjoyment—in order to take it up. By knowing precisely what you are receiving and what you are missing out on, you ought to be able to make better-informed, more reasonable decisions. Consider that most famous economic rule of all: there's no such thing as a free lunch. Even if someone offers to take you out to lunch for free, the time you will spend in the restaurant still costs you something in terms of forgone opportunities.

Some people find the idea of opportunity cost extremely discouraging: imagine spending your entire life calculating whether your time would be better spent elsewhere doing something more profitable or enjoyable. Yet, in a sense it's human nature to do precisely that— we assess the advantages and disadvantages of decisions all the time.

In the business world, a popular phrase is "value for money." People want their cash to go as far as possible. However, another is fast obtaining an advantage: "value for time." The biggest restriction on our resources is the number of hours we can devote to something, so we look to maximize the return we get on our investment of time. By reading this passage you are giving over a bit of your time which could be spent doing other activities, such as sleeping or eating. In return, however, this passage will help you to think like an economist, closely considering the opportunity cost of each of your decisions.

【2014 年大陸江蘇卷】

(　　) 1. According to the passage, the concept of "opportunity cost" is applicable to _____.
    A. making more money
    B. taking more opportunities
    C. reducing missed opportunities
    D. weighing opportunities

(　　) 2. The "leftover…time" in Paragraph 3 probably refers to the time _____.
    A. spared for watching the match at home
    B. taken to have dinner with friends
    C. spent on the way to and from the match
    D. that the match will take to play

(　　) 3. What are forgone opportunities?
    A. Opportunities you forget in decision-making.
    B. Opportunities you give up for better ones.
    C. Opportunities you miss accidentally.
    D. Opportunities you make up for.

Test 6 詳解

（2014 年大陸江蘇卷）

【第一段】

***However** wealthy we may be*, we can *never* find enough hours *in the day* *to do everything we want*.

　　無論我們多麼富有，我們都絕對無法在一天當中，找到足夠的時間，做我們想做的每一件事。

wealthy〔'wɛlθɪ〕*adj.* 有錢的
hours〔aʊrz〕*n. pl.* 時間（= *time*）

Economics deals with this problem *through the concept of opportunity cost,* **which** simply refers to **whether** someone's time **or** money could be better spent on something else.
　　　　　　名　　詞　　子　　句

經濟學透過機會成本的概念，來探討這個問題，簡單地說，這個概念是指，一個人的時間或金錢是否花在其他的事物上更好。

economics〔,ikə'namɪks〕*n.* 經濟學
deal with 應付；處理；討論　　concept〔'kansɛpt〕*n.* 概念
opportunity cost 機會成本（= *alternative cost*）【經濟學用語，
　　當你選擇一樣，放棄的另一樣，就是你的「機會成本」】
refer to 是指

【第二段】

Every hour *of our time* has a value. *For every hour we work at one job* we could *quite easily* be doing another, *or* be sleeping *or* watching a film.

我們擁有的時間，每個小時都有價值。因為我們用來工作的每個小時，都可以輕易地換做另一件事，或睡覺，或看電影。

> *for every* 每…就有 (= *for each*)
>
> 【例如】 For every three people who agree, you'll find five who don't.
>
> (每三個人同意，就有五個人不同意。)
>
> *work at* 從事；致力於 (= *work on* = *perform*)

Each *of these options* has a *different* opportunity cost—*namely, what* they cost us in missed opportunities.

這些選擇當中的每一個，都有不同的機會成本——也就是我們在所錯失的機會中付出的代價。

> 破折號 (—) 表示「解釋、說明」。【詳見「文法寶典」p.42 】
>
> option (ˈɑpʃən) *n.* 選擇 (= *choice*)
>
> namely (ˈnemlɪ) *adv.* 也就是 (= *in other words* = *that is to say*)
>
> cost (kɔst) *v.* 使付出；使喪失；花費
>
> missed (mɪst) *adj.* 錯過的

【第三段】

Say you intend to watch a football match, *but* the tickets

are expensive *and* it will take you a couple of hours *to get to*

and from the stadium.

　　比方說，你打算去看一場美式足球賽，但是門票很貴，而且你得花費幾個小時往返體育館。

> *say* *adv.* 例如；比方說【詳見「文法寶典」p.361】
> = *let's say*
> = *for example*
> = *for instance*
>
> intend〔ɪn'tɛnd〕*v.* 打算　　match〔mætʃ〕*n.* 比賽
>
> *a couple of* 幾個　　stadium〔'stedɪəm〕*n.* 體育館

Why not, you might reason, watch the game *from home and*

use the leftover money *and* time *to have dinner with friends*?

你可能這樣推論：何不在家裡看比賽，並用剩下的錢和時間去和朋友吃晚餐呢？

> 「*Why not* + 原形 V.？」作「何不～？」解，表「建議」。
>
> reason〔'rizn〕*v.* 推理
>
> leftover〔'lɛft,ovɚ〕*adj.* 剩下的；殘餘的
>
> have〔hæv〕*v.* 吃

This—*the alternative use of your cash and time*—is the
opportunity cost.

這個──使用你的錢和時間的替代方案──就是機會成本。

> alternative 〔ɔl'tɜnətɪv〕 *adj.* 可供選擇的；替代的

【第四段】

For economists, every decision is made *by knowledge of*

what one must forgo—*in terms of money* **and** *enjoyment*—*in*

order to take it up.

對於經濟學家而言，做每個決定時，都知道自己要放棄什麼──
用金錢和享樂的觀點來衡量──以做出決定。

> ***take up*** 字面的意思是「拿起來」，引申爲「採用」
> (= *adopt*)。***take it up*** 在此等於 ***make the decision***
> 「做決定」。
>
> economist〔ɪ'kɑnəmɪst〕*n.* 經濟學家
> ***make a decision*** 做決定　　knowledge〔'nɑlɪdʒ〕*n.* 知道
> forgo〔fɔr'go〕*v.* 抛棄；放棄 (= *give up* = *abandon*)
> ***in terms of*** 以…的觀點
> enjoyment〔ɪn'dʒɔɪmənt〕*n.* 快樂

*By knowing precisely **what** you are receiving **and what** you are*

名　詞　子　句

missing out on, you ought to be able to make *better-informed*,

名　詞　子　句

more reasonable decisions.

藉由精確地知道你即將要得到的，和你將錯失的，你應該能夠有更準確的資訊，做出合理的決定。

precisely〔prɪˈsaɪslɪ〕*adv.* 精確地

miss out on 錯過（ = *miss* ）

better-informed *adj.* 資訊更準確的；資訊更充足的（ = *having all the facts* ）【來自 well-informed *adj.* 消息靈通的；訊息充足的】

make better-informed*, *more reasonable decisions 做出更聰明、更合理的決定（ = *make smart, practical decisions* ）

Consider *that* *most famous economic* rule *of all*: there's no

such thing *as a free lunch*.

要考慮那最有名的經濟學原則：天下沒有白吃的午餐。

consider〔kənˈsɪdə〕*v.* 考慮

economic〔ˌikəˈnɑmɪk〕*adj.* 經濟的

Even if *someone offers to take you out to lunch for free,* the
time *you will spend in the restaurant still* costs you something
in terms of forgone opportunities.

即使某人提議要帶你出去吃免費的午餐，你在餐廳所花費的時間，就
你所放棄的機會的觀點來看，依然讓你付出了一些代價。

forgone 是 forgo（放棄）的過去分詞，作「放棄的」解。

offer〔ˋɔfɚ〕v. 提議　　**for free**　免費地（= *for nothing*）

【第五段】

Some people find the idea *of opportunity cost extremely*
discouraging: imagine spending your entire life calculating
whether *your time would be better spent elsewhere doing*
something more profitable **or** *enjoyable.*

有些人覺得機會成本的想法非常讓人失望：想像你的一生都在計算
是否你的時間，花在其他地方，去做更有利益或是愉快的事情會更好。

find 常見的意思是「發現」，這裡作「覺得；認為」解，
常用於 find + O. + O.C.「認為…（是）～」的句型。
spend + 時間/錢 + (in) + V-ing 表「花（時間、錢）做～」
解。

whether「是否」(= *if*) 引導名詞子句，做 calculating 的受詞。

extremely〔 ɪk'strimlɪ 〕 *adv.* 非常地 (= *very*)

discouraging〔 dɪs'kɝɪdʒɪŋ 〕 *adv.* 令人失望的 (= *disappointing*
= *depressing*)

imagine + *V-ing* 想像～

calculate〔'kælkjə,let 〕 *v.* 計算；推測

profitable〔'prɑfɪtəbḷ 〕 *adj.* 有利有圖的；有利益的

enjoyment〔 ɪn'dʒɔɪəbḷ 〕 *adj.* 令人愉快的

Yet, in a sense it's human nature ⌐*to do precisely that—we*

*assess the advantages **and** disadvantages of decisions all the*

time.

然而，在某個意義上而言，會做那樣的事就是人性——我們總是在評
估所做的決定的優點和缺點。

Yet 這裡是副詞，意思是「但是；然而」(= *However*)。
it 為虛主詞，真正的主詞為不定詞片語 to do…time。

in a sense 在某個意義上而言　　*human nature* 人性

precisely〔 prɪ'saɪslɪ 〕 *adv.* 恰好；正是

assess〔 ə'sɛs 〕 *v.* 評估；估計 (= *evaluate*)

advantages and disadvantages 優點和缺點 (= *pros and cons*)

all the time 一直；總是

【第六段】

In the business world, a popular phrase is "value for money." People want their cash to go *as far as possible*. *However*, another is *fast* obtaining an advantage: "value for time."

在商界，一個流行的說法是「物超所值」。人們想要他們的錢盡可能花得值得。然而，有另一個說法正在快速取得優勢：「時間效益」。

go 常見的意思是「去；走」，這裡作「被花掉；被用掉」(= *be spent*) 解。

go far 字面上是「走很遠」，引申爲「(錢) 能買很多東西；很管用」(= *go a long way*) 。

business world 商界；商場
popular〔'pɑpjələ〕*adj.* 流行的；受歡迎的
phrase〔frez〕*n.* 片語；說法
value for money 物超所值；很划算 (= *good value*)
as ~ as possible 盡可能~　　obtain〔əb'ten〕*v.* 獲得
advantage〔əd'væntɪdʒ〕*n.* 優勢

The biggest restriction *on our resources* is the number of hours *we can devote to something*, *so* we look to maximize the return *we get on our investment of time*.

我們最大的資源限制就是，我們能用於某事所花的時間，所以我們期待從投資的時間上，最大化自己得到的收益。

> look 的基本意思是「看」，這裡引申作「期待；期望」
> (= *expect* = *hope*)。
>
> return 的基本意思是「回來；返回」，這裡作「收益」
> (= *profit* = *gain*) 解。return on 表示「在⋯（得到的）收益」。
>
> restriction〔rɪ'strɪkʃən〕*n.* 限制 < *on* >
> resource〔rɪ'sors〕*n.* 資源　　number〔'nʌmbɚ〕*n.* 數量
> ***devote⋯to~*** 　將（時間、努力等）用於~
> maximize〔'mæksə,maɪz〕*v.* 使~最大化
> investment〔ɪn'vɛstmənt〕*n.* 投資

By reading this passage you are giving over a bit of your time

which could be spent doing other activities, such as sleeping or

eating.

藉由閱讀本文，你正在花你少許的時間，這些時間本來能用來做其他的活動，像是睡覺或是吃飯。

> give over⋯(to) 字面意思是「把⋯交付（給）」，引申爲「花（時間）」(= *devote*)。
>
> which 爲關代，引導形容詞子句，修飾先行詞 time。
>
> ***a bit of*** 一點點

In return, *however*, this passage will help you to think *like an*

economist, *closely considering the opportunity cost of each of*

your decisions.

然而，本文的回報是將幫助你像經濟學家一樣思考，仔細地考慮你每
個決定的成本。

> ***in return*** 作為回報　　closely〔ˋkloslɪ〕*adv.* 專心地；仔細地

1. (**D**) 根據本文，「機會成本」的概念適用於 _____ 。
   A. 賺更多的錢　　　　　　　B. 利用更多的機會
   C. 減少錯失的機會　　　　　D. 衡量機會
   applicable〔ˋæplɪkəbḷ〕*adj.* 適用…的
   reduce〔rɪˋdjus〕*v.* 減少　　weigh〔we〕*v.* 衡量

2. (**C**) 第三段的 "leftover…time" 可能是指 _____ 的時間。
   A. 挪出來在家裡看比賽　　　B. 用來和朋友吃晚餐
   C. 花在往返比賽　　　　　　D. 打比賽所花
   spare〔spɛr〕*v.* 騰出（時間）
   take〔tek〕*v.* 花費（時間）

3. (**B**) 放棄的機會是什麼？
   A. 做決定時你所忘記的機會。
   B. 為了更好的機會所放棄的機會。
   C. 你意外錯過的機會。　　　D. 你彌補的機會。
   accidentally〔͵æksəˋdɛntḷɪ〕*adv.* 意外地
   make up for 彌補

Test 7
（2014 年大陸全國新課標卷）

　　In most people's minds, a typical lion tamer（馴獸師）is an entertainer holding a whip（鞭）and a chair. The whip gets all of the attention, but it's mostly for show. In reality, it's the chair that does the important work. When a lion tamer holds a chair in front of the lion's face, the lion tries to focus on all four legs of the chair at the same time. With its focus divided, the lion becomes confused and is unsure about what to do next. When faced with so many options, the lion chooses to freeze and wait instead of attacking the man holding the chair.

　　How often do you find yourself in the same position as the lion? How often do you have something you want to achieve (e.g. lose weight, start a business, travel more)—only to end up confused by all of the options in front of you and never make progress?

This upsets me to no end because while all the experts are busy debating about which option is best, the people who want to improve their lives are left confused by all of the conflicting information. The end result is that we feel like we can't focus or that we're focused on the wrong things, and so we take less action, make less progress, and stay the same when we could be improving.

It doesn't have to be that way. Anytime you find the world waving a chair in your face, remember this: All you need to do is focus on one thing. You just need to get started. Starting before you feel ready is one of the habits of successful people. If you have somewhere you want to go, something you want to accomplish, someone you want to become...take immediate action. If you're clear about where you want to go, the rest of the world will either help you get there or get out of the way. 【2014 年大陸全國新課標卷】

(　) 1. Why does the lion tamer use a chair?

    A. To trick the lion.

    B. To show off his skills.

    C. To get ready for a fight.

    D. To entertain the audience.

(　) 2. In what sense are people similar to a lion facing a chair?

    A. They feel puzzled by choices.

    B. They hold on to the wrong things.

    C. They find it hard to make changes.

    D. They have to do something for show.

(　) 3. What is the author's attitude towards the experts mentioned in Paragraph 3?

    A. Tolerant.　　　　B. Doubtful.

    C. Respectful.　　　D. Supportive.

(　) 4. When the world is "waving a chair in your face," you're advised to _____.

    A. wait for a better chance

    B. break your old habits

    C. make a quick decision

    D. ask for clear guidance

Test 7 詳解
（2014 年大陸全國新課標卷）

【第一段】

In most people's minds, a typical lion tamer is an

entertainer *holding a whip and a chair.*

在大部分人的心目中，一位典型的馴獸師是個手握鞭子和椅子的
表演者。

> holding a whip and a chair 用來形容 an entertainer，相當
> 於 who holds a whip and chair。
>
> ***in** one's **mind*** 在某人的腦子裡；在某人的想法中
>
> 【***to** one's **mind*** 則是「依某人看來；某人認爲」】
>
> typical〔'tɪpɪk̩〕*adj.* 典型的　　tamer〔'temɚ〕*n.* 馴獸師
> entertainer〔,ɛntɚ'tenɚ〕*n.* 演藝人員　　whip〔hwɪp〕*n.* 鞭子

The whip gets all of the attention, ***but*** it's *mostly* for show.
鞭子得到所有的關注，但它多半是用來作秀的。

> ***get all the attention*** 得到所有關注；成爲焦點
> (= *take center stage* = *be in the spotlight*)
> mostly〔'mostlɪ〕*adv.* 大多　　show〔ʃo〕*n.* 秀；表演

In reality, it's the chair ***that** does the important work.*
實際上，是椅子起了重要的作用。

in reality 事實上（ = *in fact* = *actually* ）

do〔du〕*v.* 產生　　work〔wɜk〕*n.* 作用

When *a lion tamer holds a chair in front of the lion's face*, the lion tries to focus on all four legs *of the chair at the same time.*

當馴獸師在獅子的面前拿著一張椅子時，獅子會試圖把焦點同時放在椅子的四隻腳上。

focus on 聚焦於；專心於（ = *concentrate on* ）

at the same time 同時

With its focus divided, the lion becomes confused **and** is unsure about **what** to do next.

由於牠的注意力被分散，獅子變得困惑，不確定自己下一步要怎麼做。

with 可表示原因、理由，在這裡是作「因為；由於」解。

focus〔'fokəs〕*n.* 關心；注意

be unsure about 對於…沒把握（ = *be uncertain about* ）

When *faced with so many options*, the lion chooses to freeze **and** wait instead of attacking the man *holding the chair.*

當面對那麼多選擇時，獅子選擇靜止不動並等待，而非攻擊手拿椅子的男人。

When faced with… 是 When it was faced with… 的省略。
副詞子句中，句意很明顯時，可省略主詞和 be 動詞。

be faced with 面對 (= *face*)　　　　option〔ˈɑpʃən〕*n.* 選擇
freeze〔friz〕*v.* 呆立不動

【第二段】

How often do you find yourself in the same position *as
the lion*?

你有多常發現自己的處境和獅子相同？

position 常用的意思為「姿勢；位置」，在這裡的意思為
「處境」。

How *often* do you have something *you want to achieve* (*e.g.
lose weight, start a business, travel more*)—*only to end up
confused by all of the options in front of you **and** never make
progress*?
你多常有想要達成某件事（如減重、創業、更常旅遊）──最後結果
卻是對於在你面前的所有選項感到困惑，而從來就沒有任何進展？

e.g. 源自拉丁文 exempli gratia，意思為「舉例來說」。

end up 結果成為；最終成為；以…終結 (= *finish* = *wind up*)
make progress 前進；進行 (= *advance*)；進步

【第三段】

This upsets me *to no end* ***because while*** *all the experts are*

*busy debating about which option is best, the people **who** want*

to improve their lives are left confused by all of the conflicting

information.

這非常困擾我，因爲當所有專家都忙著爭論哪個選擇是最好的時候，那些想要改善生活的人，都因所有的衝突訊息而感到困惑。

(to) no end 字面上的意思是「沒有結尾」，做爲片語使用時為「繼續地；不停地」，口語使用時為「非常；許多」（ = *a lot* ）。另外，to no end 也可作「沒結果的；徒勞無功的」（ = *unavailing* ）解。

upset〔ʌpˈsɛt〕*v.* 使不高興；使心煩
be busy + V-ing 忙著…　　leave〔liv〕*v.* 使處於（某種狀態）
conflicting〔kənˈflɪktɪŋ〕*adj.* 衝突的

The end result is ***that*** *we feel like we can't focus **or that** we're*

focused on the wrong things, ***and so*** *we take less action, make*

less progress, ***and*** *stay the same **when** we could be improving.*

最終的結果是，我們感覺像是我們無法專注，或我們聚焦在錯誤的事情上，所以當我們有可能改善時，我們就比較少採取行動、比較少進步，並保持原樣。

could be... 在這裡的用法表達了推測、可能的意思。
【詳見「文法寶典」p.313, p.315】

end〔ɛnd〕*adj.* 最終的；最後的
focus〔'fokəs〕*v.* 專注；使專注
be focused on 專注於 (= *focus on*)
take action 採取行動　　stay〔ste〕*v.* 保持

【第四段】

It doesn't have to be that way. ***Anytime*** *you find the world*
waving a chair in your face, remember this: All *you need to do*
is focus on one thing.

　　它並不需要這樣子。任何時候當你發現這個世界正在你面前揮舞
著椅子，記住這一點：你所需要做的，就是專注於一件事情。

　　find 爲不完全及物動詞，之後須有受詞及受詞補語，其句型
爲 S. + V. + O. + O.C.，此種動詞常見的有：think「想」、
believe「相信」、consider「認爲」。

You just need to get started. Starting ***before*** *you feel ready* is
one of the habits *of successful people*.

　　你只需要開始。在你覺得準備好之前開始，是成功人士的習慣之一。

　　以 Starting... 開頭的動名詞片語句中做 is 的主詞。
get started 開始

[If you have somewhere you want to go, something you want to

accomplish, someone you want to become]…take immediate
action.
如果你有地方想要去，你有事情想要完成，你想要成為什麼樣的人……
就立即採取行動。

> somewhere you want to go、something you want to
> accomplish、someone you want to become 都是動詞
> have 的受詞。
>
> accomplish〔əˋkamplɪʃ〕v. 完成

*If you're clear about **where** you want to go*, the rest *of the world*

will ***either*** help you get there *or* get out of the way.
如果你清楚地了解你想去哪裡，世界上其他的人要麼會幫助你到達那
裡，或者會讓路。

> where you want to go 是以疑問代名詞 where 引導的名詞
> 子句（又稱間接問句）。
>
> ***either…or~*** 為選擇連接詞，意思是「不是…就是~」，在
> 此句中用來連接兩個動詞。【詳見「文法寶典」p.474】
>
> ***the world*** 全世界的人　　***get out of the way*** 讓路

1. (**A**) 為什麼馴獸師會使用椅子？

    A. 為了欺騙獅子。

    B. 為了炫耀他的技術。

    C. 為了準備好一場打鬥。

    D. 為了娛樂觀眾。

        trick〔trɪk〕*v.* 欺騙　　***show off*** 炫耀
        fight〔faɪt〕*v.* 戰鬥；打架

2. (**A**) 人類在哪一方面與獅子面對一張椅子相似？

    A. 他們面對選擇會感到困惑。

    B. 他們堅持錯的事情。

    C. 他們覺得做改變是困難的。

    D. 他們為了表演必須做些事。

        puzzled〔'pʌzḷd〕*adj.* 困惑的　　***hold on to*** 堅持

3. (**B**) 作者對於在第三段中所提到的專家看法為何？

    A. 容忍的。　　　　　　B. 懷疑的。

    C. 尊重的。　　　　　　D. 支持的。

        attitude〔'ætə,tjud〕*n.* 態度；看法
        tolerant〔'talərənt〕*adj.* 容忍的

4. (**C**) 當世界「在你面前揮舞著椅子」，作者建議你 ＿＿＿＿＿＿。

    A. 要等待較好的選擇

    B. 要戒除你的舊習慣

    C. 要做出明快的決定

    D. 要尋求清楚的指導

        break〔brek〕*v.* 戒除（習慣）
        guidance〔'gaɪdəns〕*n.* 指導

Test 8

（2014 年大陸北京卷）

Store Scent（香味）

What is the first thing you notice when you walk into a shop? The products displayed（展示）at the entrance? Or the soft background music?

But have you ever noticed the smell? Unless it is bad, the answer is likely to be no. But while a shop's scent may not be outstanding compared with sights and sounds, it is certainly there. And it is proving to be an increasingly powerful tool in encouraging people to purchase.

A brand store has become famous for its distinctive scent, which floats through the fairly dark hall and out to the entrance via scent machines. A smell may be attractive but it may not just be used for freshening air. One sports goods company once reported that when it first introduced scent into its stores, customers' intention to purchase increased by 80 percent.

When it comes to the best shopping streets in Paris, scent is just as important to a brand's success as the quality of its window displays and goods on sale. That is mainly because shopping is a very different experience from what it used to be.

Some years ago, the focus for brand name shopping was on a few people, who tolerated sales assistants' disapproving attitudes and don't-touch-what-you-can't-afford displays. Now the rise of electronic commerce (e-commerce) has opened up famous brands to a wider audience. But while e-shops can use sights and sounds, only brick-and-mortar stores（實體店）can offer a full experience from the minute customers step through the door to the moment they leave. Another brand store seeks to be much more than a shop, but rather a <u>destination</u>. And scent is just one way to achieve this.

Now, a famous store uses a complex man-made smell to make sure that the soft scent of baby powder floats through the kids department, and coconut（椰子）scent in the swimsuit section. A department store has even opened a new lab, inviting customers on a journey into the store's windows to smell books, pots and drawers, in search of their perfect scent.【2014 年大陸北京卷】

(　) 1. According to the passage, what is an increasingly powerful tool in the success of some brand stores?
A. Friendly assistants.　　B. Unique scents.
C. Soft background music.
D. Attractive window displays.

(　) 2. E-shops are mentioned in the passage to _____.
A. show the advantages of brick-and-mortar stores
B. urge shop assistants to change their attitude
C. push stores to use sights and sounds
D. introduce the rise of e-commerce

(　) 3. The underlined word "destination" in paragraph 5 means _____.
A. a platform that exhibits goods
B. a spot where travelers like to stay
C. a place where customers love to go
D. a target that a store expects to meet

(　) 4. The main purpose of the passage is to _____.
A. compare and evaluate
B. examine and assess　　C. argue and discuss
D. inform and explain

Test 8 詳解
（2014 年大陸北京卷）

【第一段】

Store Scent

What is the first thing you notice *when you walk into a shop*?

商店的香味

當你走進一家店時，什麼是你第一個會注意到的東西呢？

you notice 是形容詞子句，原本是 that you notice，因為 the first thing 是 notice 的受詞，所以能省略 that。另外，因為先行詞之前有 the first，所以關代較常用 that。

【詳見「文法寶典」p.153, p.155】

The products *displayed at the entrance*? *Or* the soft background music?

是那些被展示在入口的商品？或是柔和的背景音樂呢？

displayed at the entrance 是分詞片語，由形容詞子句 that are displayed at the entrance 簡化而來。

【詳見「文法寶典」p.457】

display〔dɪˈsple〕v. 展示　　entrance〔ˈɛntrəns〕n. 入口

soft〔sɔft〕*adj.*（聲音等）柔和的

background〔'bæk,graʊnd〕*n.* 背景

【第二段】

But have you *ever* noticed the smell? *Unless it is bad*, the answer is likely to be no.

　　但你可曾注意過味道？除非那個味道很差，不然答案很可能不是吧。

　　unless 表「除非」，是 if…not 的加強語氣。

【詳見「文法寶典」p.520】

smell〔smɛl〕*n.* 味道

But while a shop's scent may not be outstanding compared with sights *and* sounds, it is *certainly* there.

　　但是，雖然一家店的味道跟影像及聲音比起來，可能沒那麼突出，但它確實存在。

　　while「雖然」，引導表讓步的副詞子句。【詳見「文法寶典」p.528】

scent〔sɛnt〕*n.* 氣味；香味

outstanding〔'aʊt'stændɪŋ〕*adj.* 突出的（= *distinguished*）

compared with 和…相比　　sight〔saɪt〕*n.* 景象

And it is proving to be an *increasingly* powerful tool *in*

encouraging people to purchase.

而且它也被證明說是一個愈來愈能有效地鼓勵人們購買的工具。

　　　in 在此表「在…方面；關於」。【詳見「文法寶典」p.580】

　　　prove〔pruv〕*v.* 證實；顯示

　　　increasingly〔ɪn'krisɪŋlɪ〕*adv.* 愈來愈 (= *more and more*
　　　= *gradually*)

　　　powerful〔'pauəfəl〕*adj.* 強有力的

　　　encourage〔ɪn'kɝɪdʒ〕*n.* 鼓勵　　　purchase〔'pɝtʃəs〕*v.* 購買

【第三段】

A brand store has become famous *for its distinctive scent,*

which *floats through the fairly dark hall* ***and*** *out to the entrance*

via scent machines.

　　有家名牌店，因為它那藉由薰香機所產生的，獨特且能飄過漆黑
大廳抵達大門口的香味而著名。

　　　fairly 表「相當地」，不可與 too 或比較級連用。【詳見「文
法寶典」p.259】

　　【比較】***be famous for*** 以…（特點）而有名
　　　　　　be famous as 以…（身份、名稱）而有名
　　　　　　be famous to sb. 對某人來說很有名；被某人熟知

distinctive〔dɪ'stɪŋktɪv〕*adj.* 獨特的（ = *unique* = *special* ）

hall〔hɔl〕*n.* 大廳

via〔'vaɪə〕*prep.* 藉由（某種途徑）；透過（某種方式）

A smell may be attractive ***but*** it may not *just* be used *for*

freshening air.

味道可能會很有吸引力，但它可能不只是被用來淨化空氣。

attractive〔ə'træktɪv〕*adj.* 有吸引力的（ = *appealing* = *enticing*
= *tempting* = *alluring* ）

freshen〔'frɛʃən〕*v.* 使清新

One sports goods company *once* reported ***that when*** *it first*

introduced scent into its stores, customers' intention to purchase

increased by 80 percent.

一家運動用品公司曾經指出，當他們第一次引進香味到他們店裡時，
顧客的購買意願就增加了百分之八十。

by 在此表「差距」。【詳見「文法寶典」p.566】

sports〔sports〕*adj.* 運動的　　goods〔gʊdz〕*n. pl.* 商品

report〔rɪ'port〕*v.* 報告；說

introduce〔,ɪntrə'djus〕*v.* 介紹；引進

intention〔ɪn'tɛnʃən〕*n.* 意圖；意願

【第四段】

When *it comes to the best shopping streets in Paris*, scent is *just as* important *to a brand's success **as** the quality of its window displays **and** goods on sale.*

一提到巴黎最棒的購物街，味道對於一個品牌的成功與否的重要性，就跟櫥窗展示以及銷售的商品的品質一樣。

as…as 表「像…一樣」，第一個 as 是副詞，修飾後面的形容詞片語 important to a brand's success，第二個 as 是連接詞，引導副詞子句修飾第一個 as。而第二個 as 所引導的副詞子句常以省略句的形式出現，原本的副詞子句應該是 the quality of its window displays and goods on sale are to a brand's success.【詳見「文法寶典」p.506】

when it comes to 一提到 (= *in regard to* = *speaking of*)
on sale 出售的

That is *mainly **because** shopping is a very different experience from **what** it used to be.*

這主要是因為購物跟以前比起來，已經是個非常不一樣的經驗了。

複合關係代名詞 what 是兼做先行詞的關係代名詞，在此可代換成 the experience that。【詳見「文法寶典」p.156】

mainly〔ˋmenlɪ〕 *adv.* 主要地

【比較】*used to V.* 以前…　　*be used to V-ing* 習慣於…

be used to V. 被用來…

【第五段】

Some years ago, the focus *for brand name shopping* was on a few people, who tolerated *sales assistants' disapproving attitudes **and** don't-touch-what-you-can't-afford displays.*

好幾年前，購買名牌的焦點在少數人身上，他們忍受店員不以爲然的態度，還有那種你買不起就不要碰的展示品上。

focus〔'fokəs〕*n.* 焦點　　***brand name*** 名牌

tolerate〔'tɑlə,ret〕*v.* 忍受

assistant〔ə'sɪstənt〕*n.* 助手；助理

sales assistant 店員（= *shop assistant*）

disapproving attitude〔,dɪsə'pruvɪŋ 'ætə,tjud〕*n.* 不以爲然的態度

display〔dɪ'sple〕*n.* 展示品（= *exhibit*）

Now the rise *of electronic commerce (e-commerce)* has opened up famous brands *to a wider audience.*

現在電子商務的興起，已經將知名的品牌開放給更廣大的品牌愛好者。

rise〔raɪz〕*n.* 興起　　electronic〔ɪ,lɛk'trɑnɪk〕*adj.* 電子的

commerce〔'kɑmɝs〕*n.* 商業

electronic commerce 電子商務　　***open up*** 開放；開啓

audience〔'ɔdɪəns〕*n.* 觀衆；支持者；愛好者

But while e-shops can use sights *and* sounds, only brick-and-mortar stores can offer a full experience *from the minute customers step through the door to the moment they leave.*

雖然電子商店能夠使用聲音與影像，但只有實體店面能夠提供顧客從第一分鐘踏入店內，到最後一刻離開店的完整體驗。

e-shop *n.* 電子商店　　brick〔brɪk〕*n.* 磚頭
mortar〔'mɔrtɚ〕*n.* 灰泥　　***brick-and-mortar store*** 實體店面
offer〔'ɔfɚ〕*v.* 提供　　full〔ful〕*adj.* 完整的
step〔stɛp〕*v.* 踏出一步；前進

Another brand store seeks to be *much* more than a shop, ***but rather*** a destination.

另一家品牌店試圖要成為不僅是一家店，而是一個吸引消費者的地點。

rather 在此表「更確切的來說是…」。

seek to V. 試圖要…　　***more than*** 只是
destination〔ˏdɛstə'neʃən〕*n.* 目的地

And scent is *just* one way *to achieve this.*

而香味只是一個達到這個目標的一個方式。

achieve〔ə'tʃiv〕*v.* 達到（= *accomplish* = *attain*）

【第六段】

Now, a famous store uses a complex man-made smell *to*

*make sure **that** the soft scent of baby powder floats through the*

*kids department, **and** coconut scent in the swimsuit section.*

現在，一家有名的店使用複合的人造氣味，來確保在兒童部門飄著嬰兒爽身粉的柔和氣味，還有泳裝部門飄著椰子的清香。

complex〔kəm'plɛks〕*adj.* 複雜的（= *complicated*）；複合的；合成的　man-made〔'mæn'med〕*adj.* 人造的

make sure 確定　　***baby powder*** 嬰兒爽身粉

coconut〔'kokə,nʌt〕*n.* 椰子　　swimsuit〔'swɪm,sut〕*n.* 泳裝

A department store has *even* opened a new lab, *inviting*

customers on a journey into the store's windows to smell books,

pots and drawers, in search of their perfect scent.

一家百貨公司甚至開設了一間新的實驗室，邀請顧客進入店內的櫥窗去聞書、鍋子及抽屜，以體驗一次尋找他們自己完美味道的旅程。

in 可以用來表示目的，此用法常會使用「in + 名詞 + 介系詞」的形式。【詳見「文法寶典」p.581】

inviting customers... 是分詞構句。當對等子句主詞相同時，保留一主詞即可。原本的句子是 and it invited customers...。【詳見「文法寶典」p.459】

lab〔læb〕*n.* 實驗室（= *laboratory*）

journey〔'dʒɜnɪ〕*n.* 旅程　　pot〔pɑt〕*n.* 鍋子

drawer〔'drɔɚ〕*n.* 抽屜　　***in search of*** 尋找

1. (**B**) 根據本文，在一些品牌店的成功案例中，什麼是愈來愈有力的工具？
   A. 友善的店員。　　　　　B. 獨特的氣味。
   C. 柔和的背景音樂。　　　D. 吸引人的櫥窗展示。
   unique〔ju'nik〕*adj.* 獨特的

2. (**A**) 電子商店在本文中被提及是爲了要 _____。
   A. 證明實體店的優勢　　　B. 鞭策店員改變他們的態度
   C. 催促店家使用影像與聲音　D. 介紹電子商務的興起
   urge〔ɜdʒ〕*v.* 催促；力勸　　push〔puʃ〕*v.* 催促；驅使

3. (**C**) 在第五段中畫底線的 "destination" 的意思是 _____。
   A. 一個展示商品的平台　　B. 一個遊客喜歡待的地點
   C. 一個消費者喜歡去的地方　D. 一家店希望達到的目標
   platform〔'plæt,fɔrm〕*n.* 平台　　spot〔spɑt〕*n.* 地點
   target〔'tɑrgɪt〕*n.* 目標　　meet〔mit〕*v.* 達到（目標）

4. (**D**) 本文的主旨是要 _____。
   A. 對比並評估　　　　　B. 檢測並評估
   C. 爭論並討論　　　　　D. 告知並解釋
   evaluate〔ɪ'væljʊ,et〕*v.* 評估
   examine〔ɪg'zæmɪn〕*v.* 檢查
   assess〔ə'sɛs〕*v.* 評估　　argue〔'ɑrgju〕*v.* 爭論
   inform〔ɪn'fɔrm〕*v.* 通知；告知

Test 9
（2014 年大陸浙江卷）

Here is some must-know information from a handbook on how people behave when doing business in some countries.

In Brazil

Brazilians are warm and friendly. They often stand close when talking, and it is common for them to touch the other person on the shoulder. People often greet each other (particularly women) with light cheek kisses. Schedules tend to be flexible, with business meetings sometimes starting later than planned. But to be safe, be on time. Meals can stretch for hours—there's no such thing as rushing a meal in Brazil. Lunches also can start in the mid to late afternoon. Brazilians are social, preferring face-to-face communication over emails or phone calls.

In Singapore

Singaporeans shakes hands when they meet and often also greet each other with a small, polite bow. Business cards should be offered and received with two hands. Arriving late is considered disrespectful. So be on time. Efficiency（效率）is the goal, so meetings and dealings often are fast-paced. Singaporeans are direct in their discussions, even when the subject is money. Rank is important and authority is respected. This determines how people interact in meetings. For example, people avoid disagreeing outright with someone of a higher rank.

In the United Arab Emirates

In the UAE, status is important, so the most senior or oldest should be greeted first with their titles. The handshake seems to be longer than elsewhere. So do not pull away from a handshake. Women should cover themselves when it comes to dress. Men also tend to be covered from neck to elbows（肘部）and down to the knees. People do not avoid entertaining in their homes, but they also hold business meals at restaurants. Touching or passing food or eating with your left hand is to be avoided. When meetings are one-to-one, if your host offers you coffee, you should refuse. It might seem odd, but it is part of the culture. Coffee should only be accepted if it is already set out or presented.

In Switzerland

The Swiss tend to be formal and address each other by last name. They are also respectful of private lives. You should be careful not to ask about personal topics. Punctuality（守時）is vital, something that comes from a deep respect for others' time. Arrive at any meeting or event a few minutes early to be safe. They also have a clear structure in their companies. Higher-ups make the final decisions, even if others might disagree. Neat,

clean dress is expected. The Swiss follow formal
table manners. They also keep their hands visible at
the table and their elbows off the table. It is polite
to finish the food on your plate. 【2014年大陸浙江卷】

(　　) 1. The passage is mainly about _____.
　　　　A. communication types
　　　　B. the workplace atmosphere
　　　　C. customs and social manners
　　　　D. living conditions and standards

(　　) 2. Why do Singaporeans avoid arguing with
　　　　their boss?
　　　　A. They put efficiency in first place.
　　　　B. They dislike face-to-face communication.
　　　　C. They want to finish meetings as quickly
　　　　　 as possible.
　　　　D. They are supposed to obey the person of
　　　　　 a higher rank.

(　) 3. In the UAE, when should you refuse the
coffee if it is offered?

A. When greeting senior.

B. When meeting the host alone.

C. When attending a presentation.

D. When dining with business partners.

(　) 4. In which country do people care about where
to put their hands at the dinner table?

A. In Brazil.

B. In Singapore.

C. In the United Arab Emirates.

D. In Switzerland.

Test 9 詳解
（2014 年大陸浙江卷）

【第一段】

Here is some must-know information *from a handbook on*

***how** people behave when doing business in some countries.*

以下這些必知的訊息，是來自一本手冊，探討在某些國家做生意時大家會如何表現。

how people… 的 how 是從屬連接詞，引導名詞子句做介系詞 on 的受詞。

must-know〔'mʌst,no〕*adj.* 必知的

handbook〔'hænd,bʊk〕*n.* 手冊；指南（= *guidebook* = *manual*）

on〔ɑn〕*prep.* 關於（= *about*）

behave〔bɪ'hev〕*v.* 行為；表現　***do business*** 做生意

【第二段】

In Brazil
在巴西

Brazilians are warm and friendly. They *often* stand *close*

***when** talking*, **and** it is common *for them* to touch the other

person *on the shoulder*.

　　巴西人熱情且友善。當他們說話時，常常站得靠近，而且他們觸碰另一個人的肩膀是常見的。

Brazil〔brəˈzɪl〕*n.* 巴西　　Brazilian〔ˌbrəˈzɪljən〕*n.* 巴西人
warm〔wɔrm〕*adj.* 熱心的　　close〔klos〕*adv.* 靠近地
touch sb. on the shoulder 碰某人的肩膀

People *often* greet each other (*particularly women*) *with light cheek kisses.* Schedules tend to be flexible, *with business meetings sometimes starting later **than** planned.* ***But** to be safe,* be on time.

人們（尤其是女人），常以輕觸臉頰的親吻相互問候。時間表往往是有彈性的，有時商務會議會比原本計劃的晚開始。但爲了保險起見，就準時到吧。

　　with 表「附帶狀態」，其用法爲：

with + 受詞 + { V-ing（表主動）
　　　　　　 { p.p.（表被動）

greet〔grit〕*v.* 向⋯問候；和⋯打招呼
light〔laɪt〕*adj.* 輕的　　cheek〔tʃik〕*n.* 臉頰
schedule〔ˈskɛdʒul〕*n.* 時間表
tend to 易於；傾向於（= *be inclined to*）
flexible〔ˈflɛksəbḷ〕*adj.* 有彈性的
on time 準時

Meals can stretch *for hours*—there's no *such* thing *as rushing*

a meal in Brazil. Lunches *also* can start *in the mid to late*

afternoon.

用餐時間可以拉長到幾個小時——在巴西沒有趕忙吃完一頓飯的這種
事情。午餐也可能從下午三點左右開始直到傍晚。

> *no **such** thing **as*** 的 such…as 為解釋連接詞，表示原因或舉
> 例。
>
> stretch〔strɛtʃ〕*v.* 延伸；延續
>
> rush〔rʌʃ〕*v.* 趕緊做；倉促完成　　　mid〔mɪd〕*adj.* 中間的
>
> ***mid afternoon*** 下午三點左右（= *midafternoon*）
>
> ***late afternoon*** 傍晚

Brazilians are social, preferring face-to-face communication

*over emails **or** phone calls*.

巴西人是喜歡交際的，他們比較喜歡面對面的溝通勝過用電子郵件或
電話。

> 當兩個句子主詞相同時，為精簡句子並變化句型就可使用分
> 詞構句。此句為強調主動進行的 V-ing 分詞構句：S + V. ,
> V-ing 分詞構句。原本的兩句話為 Brazilians are social.
> Brazilians prefer face-to-face communication over emails

or phone calls. 兩句有因果關係，以連接詞連接兩句後，
變成 Brazilians are social, so they prefer face-to-face
communication over emails or phone calls. 一句話。因爲主
詞都是 Brazilians，當去掉連接兩句的連接詞 so、去掉表因
果那句的主詞和把去掉的主詞後主動執行該句的動詞改爲
preferring，強調主動進行的 V-ing 分詞構句就完成了。

【第三段】

In Singapore
在新加坡

Singaporeans shakes hands *when they meet* **and** *often also
greet each other with a small, polite bow.*

當新加坡人見面時，他們會握手，而且通常還會互相微微地、禮
貌地鞠躬問候。

Singaporean〔ˌsɪŋgəˈporɪən〕*n.* 新加坡人

Business cards should be offered **and** received *with two hands.*

Arriving *late* is considered disrespectful. **So** be on time.
要給人名片和收取名片時，應該用雙手。遲到被視爲失禮。所以要準
時。

business card 名片　　**be considered** (**to be**) 被認爲是
disrespectful〔ˌdɪsrɪˈspɛktfəl〕*adj.* 失禮的

Efficiency is the goal, *so* meetings *and* dealings *often* are

fast-paced. Singaporeans are direct *in their discussions, even*

when the subject is money.

因為效率是目標，所以會議和交易通常是快節奏的。新加坡人是直接
了當地討論，即使討論的主題是錢。

> efficiency〔əˈfɪʃənsɪ〕*n.* 效率
>
> dealings〔ˈdilɪŋz〕*n. pl.* 交易；買賣
>
> fast-paced〔ˈfæstˈpest〕*adj.* 快步調的；快節奏的

Rank is important *and* authority is respected. This determines

how people interact in meetings.

階級是重要的，而且權威是備受尊重的。這決定了人們在會議中如何
互動。

> this 為指示代名詞，可代替前面所提過的片語、子句或句
> 子，以避免重複。
>
> rank〔ræŋk〕*n.* 階級　　authority〔əˈθɔrətɪ〕*n.* 權威
>
> determine〔dɪˈtɝmɪn〕*v.* 決定　　interact〔ˌɪntɚˈækt〕*v.* 互動

For example, people avoid disagreeing *outright with someone*

of a higher rank.

例如，大家會避免當場與階級較高的人意見不合。

for example（例如）為用來舉例說明的轉承語，也可用 for instance 代換。

outright〔'aut,raɪt〕主要意思是「全部地；徹底地」，這裡作「當場；立即」解。

disagree〔,dɪsə'gri〕*v.* 意見不合 *< with >*

【第四段】

In the United Arab Emirates
在阿拉伯聯合大公國

In the UAE, status is important, *so* the *most* senior *or* oldest should be greeted *first with their titles*.

　　在阿拉伯聯合大公國，因為身份是重要的，所以最資深或最年長的人應以他們的稱謂先被問候。

Arab〔'ærəb〕*adj.* 阿拉伯的　　emirate〔ə'mɪrɪt〕*n.* 酋長國
the United Arab Emirates 阿拉伯聯合大公國；阿拉伯聯合酋長國
【簡稱「阿聯酋」】（= *the URA*）
status〔'stetəs〕*n.* 地位　　senior〔'sinjə〕*adj.* 資深的
title〔'taɪtl̩〕*n.* 頭銜；稱號

The handshake seems to be longer *than* elsewhere. *So* do not pull *away from a handshake*.

握手的時間似乎比其他地方更長。所以不要從握手當中抽離。

> seem 爲不完全不及物動詞，此類動詞之後沒有受詞，但一
> 定要有主詞補語，對主詞加以補充說明，而與主詞補語間的
> to be 有無均可。

handshake〔ˈhændˌʃek〕*n.* 握手
pull away from 撤回 (= *pull back from* = *withdraw from*)

Women should cover themselves *when it comes to dress.*

Men *also* tend to be covered *from neck to elbows* *and* down to

the knees.

當談到穿著打扮時，婦女應該著把自己包覆起來。男人也傾向於穿著
從脖子蓋到手肘，並下至膝蓋的服裝。

> ***when it comes to*** 一提到 (= *speaking about*)
> elbow〔ˈɛlˌbo〕*n.* 手肘　　knee〔ni〕*n.* 膝蓋

People do not avoid entertaining *in their homes*, *but* they *also*

hold business meals *at restaurants*. Touching *or* passing food

or eating *with your left hand* is to be avoided.

人們不會避免在自己家款待客人，但他們也是會在餐廳舉行商務會餐。
碰觸、傳遞食物，或吃東西，要避免用左手。

> pass 主要意思是「經過；穿過」，這裡作「傳遞」解。

entertain〔͵ɛntɚˈten〕v. 娛樂；招待

*When meetings are one-to-one, **if** your host offers you coffee,*
you should refuse. It might seem odd, ***but*** it is part of the
culture. Coffee should *only* be accepted ***if*** *it is already set*
*out **or** presented.*

當會議是一對一時，如果你的主人要提供咖啡給你，你應該拒絕。這
似乎很奇怪，但它是文化的一部份。咖啡應該只有在已經被擺放出來，
或遞給你時才接受。

set out 主要意思是「動身；開始」，這裡作「放置；擺放」解。

host〔host〕n. 主人　　offer〔ˈɔfɚ〕v. 提供
refuse〔rɪˈfjuz〕v. 拒絕　　odd〔ɑd〕adj. 奇怪的（= *strange*）
present〔prɪˈzɛnt〕v. 遞給

【第五段】

In Switzerland
在瑞士

The Swiss tend to be formal ***and*** address each other *by*
last name. They are also respectful of private lives. You
should be careful not to ask about personal topics.

瑞士人傾向於正式和稱呼彼此的姓氏。他們也尊重別人的私生活。你
應該小心，不要問關於個人私事的話題。

> Switzerland〔'swɪtsələnd〕*n.* 瑞士
> ***the Swiss*** 瑞士人
> formal〔'fɔrml̩〕*adj.* 正式的
> address〔ə'drɛs〕*v.* 稱呼
> ***last name*** 姓　　***first name*** 名字
> ***be respectful of*** 尊敬
> personal〔'pɝsn̩l̩〕*adj.* 涉及個人私事的

Punctuality is vital, something ***that*** *comes from a deep respect*

for others' time.　Arrive at any meeting ***or*** event *a few minutes*

early to be safe.

守時是至關重要的，這是來自於對別人時間的深深尊重。爲了安全起
見，要早幾分鐘到達任何會議或活動。

> punctuality〔ˌpʌŋktʃʊ'ælətɪ〕*n.* 守時
> vital〔'vaɪtl̩〕*adj.* 非常重要的
> event〔ɪ'vɛnt〕*n.* 大型活動

They ***also*** have a clear structure *in their companies*.　Higher-ups

make the final decisions, ***even if*** *others might disagree*.

他們在公司也有清楚的組織結構。上級會做出最終決定，即使其他人可能不同意。

> structure〔ˈstrʌkʃə〕*n.* 結構；構造；組織
> higher-up〔ˈhaɪəˌʌp〕*n.* 上級　　***even if*** 即使

Neat, clean dress is expected.
整潔、乾淨的衣服是被期待的。

> neat〔nit〕*adj.* 整潔的

The Swiss follow formal table manners. They *also* keep their hands visible *at the table* **and** their elbows *off the table.* It is polite to finish the food *on your plate.*
瑞士人會遵循正式的餐桌禮儀。他們雙手會放在餐桌上讓人看見，而手肘則不會架在桌上。吃完你盤子裡的食物才是有禮貌的。

> keep 爲不完全及物動詞，此類動詞之後須有受詞，還要有受詞補語，此句中以 and 連接 their hands visible at the table 及 their elbows off the table 這兩組受詞和受詞補語。It 爲虛主詞，代替後面的不定詞片語。
>
> follow〔ˈfalo〕*v.* 遵守　　***table manners*** 餐桌禮儀
> visible〔ˈvɪzəbḷ〕*adj.* 看得見的
> plate〔plet〕*n.* 盤子　　finish〔ˈfɪnɪʃ〕*v.* 吃光

1. (**C**) 本文主要是關於 _____ 。
    A. 溝通的類型
    B. 工作場合的氣氛
    C. 習俗和社會禮儀
    D. 生活狀況和生活水準
    workplace (ˈwɝkˌples) *n.* 工作場所
    atmosphere (ˈætməsˌfɪr) *n.* 氣氛
    standard (ˈstændəd) *n.* 水準

2. (**D**) 為什麼新加坡人避免與他們的老闆爭論？
    A. 他們把效率擺第一。
    B. 他們不喜歡面對面的溝通。
    C. 他們想盡快結束會議。
    D. 他們應該服從階級較高的人。
    be supposed to 應該　　obey (oˈbe) *v.* 服從

3. (**B**) 在阿拉伯聯合大公國，什麼時候你應該拒絕被提供咖啡？
    A. 當跟長者問好時。
    B. 當獨自和主人見面時。
    C. 當出席一場簡報時。
    D. 當與生意伙伴用餐時。
    senior (ˈsinjə) *n.* 年長者　　attend (əˈtɛnd) *v.* 參加
    presentation (ˌprɛznˈteʃən) *n.* 報告
    dine (daɪn) *v.* 用餐

4. (**D**) 在哪個國家，人們會在意在餐桌上自己的手該擺在哪裡？
    A. 在巴西。
    B. 在新加坡。
    C. 在阿拉伯聯合大公國。
    D. 在瑞士。
    care bout 在意

Test 10
（2014 年大陸遼寧卷）

A new study shows students who write notes by hand during lectures perform better on exams than those who use laptops（筆記本電腦）.

Students are increasingly using laptops for note-taking because of speed and legibility（清晰度）. But the research has found laptop users are less able to remember and apply the concepts they have been taught.

Researchers performed experiments that aimed to find out whether using a laptop increased the tendency to make notes "mindlessly" by taking down word for word what the professors said.

In the first experiment, students were giving either a laptop or pen and paper. They listened to the same lectures and were told to use their usual note-taking skills. Thirty minutes after the talk, they were examined on their ability to remember facts and on how well they understood concepts.

The researchers found that laptop users took twice as many notes as those who wrote by hand. However, the typists performed worse at remembering and applying the concepts. Both groups scored similarly when it came to memorizing facts.

The researchers' report said, "While more notes are beneficial, if the notes are taken mindlessly, as is more likely the case on a laptop, the benefit disappears."

In another experiment aimed at testing long-term memory, students took notes as before but were tested a week after the lecture. This time, the students who wrote notes by hand performed significantly better on the exam.

These two experiments suggest that handwritten notes are not only better for immediate learning and understanding, but that they also lead to superior revision in the future. 【2014 年大陸遼寧卷】

(   ) 1. More and more students favor laptops for note-taking because they can _____.

    A. write more notes

    B. digest concepts better

    C. get higher scores

    D. understand lectures better

(   ) 2. While taking notes, laptop users tend to be _____.

    A. skillful   B. mindless

    C. thoughtful   D. tireless

(   ) 3. The author of the passage aims to _____.

    A. examine the importance of long-term memory

    B. stress the benefit of taking notes by hand

    C. explain the process of taking notes

    D. promote the use of laptops

(   ) 4. The passage is likely to appear in _____.

    A. a newspaper advertisement

    B. a computer textbook

    C. a science magazine

    D. a finance report

Test 10 詳解

（2014 年大陸遼寧卷）

【第一段】

A new study shows *students **who** write notes by hand during lectures perform better on exams **than** those **who** use laptops.*

一個新的研究顯示，聽講時用手抄筆記的學生，考試時比用筆記型電腦抄筆記的學生表現得還要好。

those who 可以替換成 the people who，後面要加複數動詞。【詳見「文法寶典」p.123】

study〔ˈstʌdɪ〕*n.* 研究　　notes〔nots〕*n. pl.* 筆記

lecture〔ˈlɛktʃɚ〕*n.* 講課

perform〔pɚˈfɔrm〕*v.* 表現

laptop〔ˈlæpˌtɑp〕*n.* 筆記型電腦（= *personal computer*）

【第二段】

Students are *increasingly* using laptops *for note-taking because of speed and legibility.*

由於速度以及清晰度，漸漸地學生都使用筆記型電腦來做筆記。

because of 表「由於」，後面加上名詞或動名詞，可以代
換成 as a result of 或 owing to。

increasingly〔 ɪn'krisɪŋlɪ 〕*adv.* 逐漸地；越來越
（= *more and more*）

speed〔'spid 〕*n.* 速度

legibility〔ˌlɛdʒə'bɪlətɪ 〕*n.* 清晰度（= *clearness*）

But the research has found *laptop users are less able to*

*remember **and** apply the concepts they have been taught.*
但研究發現，使用筆記型電腦的人比較不能記得，而且應用他們被教
過的觀念。

research〔'risɝtʃ 〕*n.* 研究

be able to V. 能夠…（= *be capable of* + *V-ing*）

apply〔 ə'plaɪ 〕*v.* 應用

concept〔'kɑnsɛpt 〕*n.* 觀念（= *idea*）

【第三段】

Researchers performed experiments *that aimed to find*

*out **whether** using a laptop increased the tendency to make*

*notes "mindlessly" by taking down word for word **what** the*

professors said.

研究者做了實驗，目標在於找出使用筆記型電腦，是否會增加一字一句記錄教授說的話時，做筆記心不在焉的趨勢。

whether 引導名詞子句做 find out 的受詞。

【詳見「文法寶典」p.485】

perform〔pə'fɔrm〕*v.* 執行；做
aim to 目標在於　　*find out* 查明
tendency〔'tɛndənsɪ〕*n.* 趨勢
mindlessly〔'maɪndlɪslɪ〕*adv.* 心不在焉地
take down 記錄；寫下 (= *write down* = *record*)
word for word 逐字逐句地
professor〔prə'fɛsə〕*n.* 教授

【第四段】

In the first experiment, students were giving *either* a laptop *or* pen *and* paper.

在第一個實驗中，學生被給了筆記型電腦或者紙和筆。

either...or 表「不是…就是」，連接對等的單字、片語或子句，搭配動詞時動詞要和第二個主詞一致。

【詳見「文法寶典」p.474】

They listened to the same lectures *and* were told to use their usual note-taking skills.

他們聽了相同的講課，而且被告知要使用他們平常做筆記的技巧。

usual〔'juʒʊəl〕*adj.* 平常的 (= *common* = *typical*)

Thirty minutes after the talk, they were examined on their ability to remember facts *and* on *how well* they understood concepts.

授課三十分鐘後，他們被檢視他們在記憶事實和理解觀念的能力。

> talk〔tɔk〕*n.* 演講　　examine〔ɪgˈzæmɪn〕*v.* 檢查（= *test*）
> ability〔əˈbɪlətɪ〕*n.* 能力（= *capability* = *capacity*）

【第五段】

The researchers found *that* laptop users took twice *as many* notes *as those **who** wrote by hand.*

研究者發現，使用筆記型電腦的人，比那些用手寫記筆記的人，多記了一倍的筆記。

> as...as 表「像…一樣」，第一個 as 是副詞，修飾後面的形容詞 many，第二個 as 是連接詞，引導副詞子句修飾第一個 as。而第二個 as 所引導的副詞子句常以省略句的形式出現，原本的副詞子句應該是 those who wrote by hand took。【詳見「文法寶典」p.506】

However, the typists performed *worse at remembering **and** applying the concepts.*

然而，那些打字的人在記憶與應用概念上，表現得比較差。

typist〔'taɪpɪst〕*n.* 打字的人

Both groups scored *similarly **when** it came to memorizing facts.*

但一提到記憶事實這方面，兩組人的得分很接近。

score〔skor〕*v.* 得分
similarly〔'sɪmələlɪ〕*adv.* 類似地 (= *evenly*)
when it comes to 一提到 (= *speaking of*)
memorize〔'mɛmə,raɪz〕*v.* 記憶；背誦

【第六段】

The researchers' report said, "*While more notes are*

*beneficial, **if** the notes are taken mindlessly, **as** is more likely*

the case on a laptop, the benefit disappears."

研究人員的報導指出：「雖然多的筆記是有益的，但如果筆記是
不專心地被記下，用筆記型電腦較可能如此，這個好處就會消失。」

while 在此作「雖然」解。【詳見「文法寶典」p.528】
as 在此是關係代名詞，代替前面一整句話。
　【詳見「文法寶典」p.533】

beneficial〔,bɛnə'fɪʃəl〕*adj.* 有益的 (= *helpful* = *advantageous*)
take notes 做筆記　　benefit〔'bɛnəfɪt〕*n.* 益處
disappear〔,dɪsə'pɪr〕*v.* 消失 (= *vanish*)

【第七段】

In another experiment aimed at testing long-term memory, students took notes *as before **but*** were tested *a week after the lecture.*

　　在另一個目標是測試長期記憶的實驗，學生像之前那樣做筆記，但是在講課一週後才被測驗。

　　long-term〔͵lɔŋˋtɝm〕*adj.* 長期的

This time, the students *who wrote notes by hand* performed *significantly better on the exam.*

　　這一次，那些用手寫筆記的學生，在考試中表現得明顯比較好。

　　significantly〔sɪgˋnɪfəkəntlɪ〕*adv.* 顯著地

【第八段】

　　These two experiments suggest ***that*** *handwritten notes* *are not only better for immediate learning **and** understanding,* ***but that*** *they also lead to superior revision in the future.*

　　這兩個實驗顯示，手寫筆記不只是對立即的學習跟理解比較好，而且對於未來的複習也是比較好的。

　　superior 本身已經有比較級的概念，因此若要表達「比…好」，須使用 be superior to，意同 be better than。

suggest〔səgˋdʒɛst〕v. 顯示　　***handwritten notes*** 手寫的筆記

immediate〔ɪˋmidɪɪt〕*adj.* 立即的

lead to 導致（= *result in* = *contribute to* = *give rise to*

= *bring about*）　　superior〔səˋpɪrɪɚ〕*adj.* 較好的

revision〔rɪˋvɪʒən〕*n.* 複習；修正

1.（**A**）有愈來愈多學生偏好用筆記型電腦做筆記，因為他們能夠

　　　　＿＿＿＿＿。

　　　A. 寫更多筆記　　　　　　B. 更能消化觀念

　　　C. 得到更高的分數　　　　D. 更容易理解講課內容

　　　　favor〔ˋfevɚ〕*v.* 偏愛　　digest〔daɪˋdʒɛst〕*v.* 消化

　　　　score〔skor〕*n.* 分數

2.（**B**）在做筆記的時候，使用筆記型電腦的人通常會比較 ＿＿＿＿＿。

　　　A. 熟練　　B. 不專心　　C. 體貼　　D. 不疲倦

　　　　tend to V. 易於；傾向於

　　　　thoughtful〔ˋθɔtfəl〕*adj.* 體貼的

　　　　tireless〔ˋtaɪrlɪs〕*adj.* 不疲倦的

3.（**B**）本文作者的目的是要 ＿＿＿＿＿。

　　　A. 要檢視長期記憶的重要性　　B. 強調手寫筆記的好處

　　　C. 解釋記筆記的過程　　　　　D. 提倡使用筆記型電腦

4.（**C**）這篇文章最可能出現在 ＿＿＿＿＿。

　　　A. 報紙的廣告　　　　　　B. 電腦教科書

　　　C. 科學雜誌　　　　　　　D. 財務報告

　　　　textbook〔ˋtɛkt͵bʊk〕*n.* 教科書

　　　　finance〔fəˋnæns〕*n.* 財務

Test 11
（2014 年大陸全國新課標卷）

As more and more people speak the global languages of English, Chinese, Spanish, and Arabic, other languages are rapidly disappearing. In fact, half of the 6,000-7,000 languages spoken around the world today will likely die out by the next century, according to the United Nations Educational, Scientific, and Cultural Organization (UNESCO).

In an effort to prevent language loss, scholars from a number of organizations—UNESCO and National Geographic among them—have for many years been documenting dying languages and the cultures they reflect.

Mark Turin, a scientist at the Macmillan Center, Yale University, who specializes in the languages and oral traditions of the Himalayas, is following in <u>that tradition</u>. His recently published book, *A Grammar of Thangmi with an Ethnolinguistic Introduction to the Speakers and Their Culture*, grew out of his experience living, working, and raising a family in a village in Nepal.

Documenting the Thangmi language and culture is just a starting point for Turin, who seeks to include other languages and oral traditions across the Himalayan reaches of India, Nepal, Bhutan, and China. But he is not content to simply record these voices before they disappear without record.

At the University of Cambridge, Turin discovered a wealth of important materials—including photographs, films, tape recordings, and field notes—which had remained unstudied and were badly in need of care and protection.

Now, through the two organizations that he has founded—the Digital Himalaya Project and the World Oral Literature Project—Turin has started a campaign to make such documents, found in libraries and stores around the world, available not just to scholars but to the descendants of the communities that the materials were originally collected from. Thanks to digital technology and the widely available Internet, Turin notes, the endangered languages can be saved and reconnected with speech communities. 【2014 年大陸全國新課標卷】

(　) 1. Many scholars are making efforts to _____.
　　　A. promote global languages
　　　B. rescue disappearing languages
　　　C. search for language communities
　　　D. set up language research organizations

(　) 2. What does "that tradition" in Paragraph 3
　　　refer to?
　　　A. Creating records of the languages and
　　　　cultures.
　　　B. Writing books on language teaching.
　　　C. Telling stories about language users.
　　　D. Living with the native speakers.

(　) 3. What is Turin's book based on?
　　　A. Cultural studies in India.
　　　B. The documents available at Yale.
　　　C. His language research in Bhutan.
　　　D. His personal experience in Nepal.

(　) 4. Which of the following best describes Turin's
　　　work?
　　　A. Write, sell and donate.
　　　B. Record, repair and reward.
　　　C. Collect, protect and reconnect.
　　　D. Design, experiment and report.

Test 11 詳解
(2014 年大陸全國新課標卷)

【第一段】

As more and more people speak the global languages of

English, Chinese, Spanish, and Arabic, other languages are

rapidly disappearing.

隨著愈來愈多人說像是英文、中文、西班牙文和阿拉伯文這些世界語言，其他的語言正迅速地在消失當中。

global languages 指那些在世界上被廣泛使用的語言。

other languages 可以改爲 others。

global〔'globḷ〕*adj.* 全球的　　Arabic〔ə'ræbɪk〕*n.* 阿拉伯文
rapidly〔'ræpɪdlɪ〕*adv.* 快速地
disappear〔͵dɪsə'pɪr〕*v.* 消失（= *vanish*）

In fact, half *of the 6,000-7,000 languages spoken around the*

world today will *likely* die out *by the next century, according*

to the United Nations Educational, Scientific, and Cultural

Organization (*UNESCO*).

事實上，根據聯合國教科文組織的說法，現今六千至七千種在世界各地被說的語言中，有一半很有可能到了下一個世紀就會消失了。

> spoken around the world today 是分詞片語，是由 that are spoken around the world today 簡化而來。
>
> 【詳見「文法寶典」p.457】
>
> ***die out*** 滅絕；消失
> ***the United Nations Educational, Scientific, and Cultural Organization*** 聯合國教科文組織（= *UNESCO*〔juˋnɛsko〕）

【第二段】

In an effort to prevent language loss, scholars *from a number of organizations—UNESCO and National Geographic among them*—have *for many years* been documenting dying languages ***and*** the cultures *they reflect.*

為了要努力防止語言的流失，許多組織，像是聯合國教科文組織跟國家地理學會的學者，多年來都一直在記錄正在消失的語言以及它們所反映的文化。

> have for many years been documenting... 原本的句子是 have been documenting for many years...，將 many years 在前面，強調已經記錄了「很多年」。
>
> have for many years been documenting...使用「現在完成進行式」，表示從過去某時開始一直持續到現在仍在進行的動作。【詳見「文法寶典」p.349】

in an effort to V. 努力去做…

loss〔lɔs〕*n.* 喪失　　scholar〔'skɑlə〕*n.* 學者

a number of 好幾個

geographic〔͵dʒiə'græfɪk〕*adj.* 地理的

among〔ə'mʌŋ〕*prep.* 爲…中之一

document〔'dɑkjə͵mɛnt〕*v.* 記錄

dying〔'daɪɪŋ〕*adj.* 垂死的

reflect〔rɪ'flɛkt〕*v.* 反映

【第三段】

Mark Turin, *a scientist at the Macmillan Center, Yale*

University, **who** *specializes in the languages* **and** *oral traditions*

of the Himalayas, is following in that tradition.

　　馬克・圖靈，一位在耶魯大學麥克米倫中心工作，且專精於喜馬
拉雅山語言跟口語傳統的科學家，正在遵循那個傳統。

　　, who specializes in… 是形容詞子句，因爲是補述用法用
以補充說明 Mark Turin，所以要加上逗點。

　　【詳見「文法寶典」p.161, p.162】

specialize in 專精於　　oral〔'ɔrəl〕*adj.* 口頭的

tradition〔trə'dɪʃən〕*n.* 傳統

follow in 遵循

the Himalayas〔hɪ'mɑljəz〕*n.* 喜馬拉雅山脈

His *recently* published book, *A Grammar of Thangmi with an Ethnolinguistic Introduction to the Speakers and Their Culture*, grew out of his experience living, working, ***and*** raising a family *in a village in Nepal*.

他最近出版的書籍《唐米語文法及說話者與他們文化的人類語言學入門》，是由他在尼泊爾一個村莊生活、工作，及養育子女的經驗而寫成的。

recently〔ˈrisn̩tlɪ〕*adv.* 最近　　publish〔ˈpʌblɪʃ〕*v.* 出版

grammar〔ˈɡræmɚ〕*n.* 文法

Thangmi〔ˈteŋmɪ〕*n.* 唐米語

ethnolinguistic〔ˌɛθnəlɪŋˈɡwɪstɪk〕*adj.* 人類語言學的

introduction〔ˌɪntrəˈdʌkʃən〕*n.* 介紹；簡介

grow out of 產生於　　raise〔rez〕*v.* 養育；撫養

raise a family 養育子女　　village〔ˈvɪlɪdʒ〕*n.* 村莊

Nepal〔nɪˈpɔl〕*n.* 尼泊爾

【第四段】

Documenting the Thangmi language ***and*** culture is just a starting point *for Turin*, ***who*** *seeks to include other languages* ***and*** *oral traditions across the Himalayan reaches of India, Nepal, Bhutan,* ***and*** *China.*

記錄唐米語和文化，對圖靈這位試圖包含其他遍及喜馬拉雅地區，如印度、尼泊爾、不丹跟中國，語言及口語傳統的人來說，只是一個起始點。

> , who seeks to... 是形容詞子句，因為是補述用法用以補充說明 Mark Turin，所以要加上逗點。【詳見「文法寶典」p.161, p.162】
>
> ***starting point*** 起始點　　seek〔sik〕*n.* 尋求
> across〔əˈkrɔs〕*prep.* 遍及
> Himalayan〔hɪˈmɑljən〕*n.* 喜馬拉雅（山脈）的
> reach〔ritʃ〕*n.* 區域　　Bhutan〔buˈtɑn〕*n.* 不丹

But he is not content to *simply* record these voices *before they disappear without record.*

但他並不滿足於只是在這些聲音沒有記錄地消失之前記錄它們。

【第五段】

At the University of Cambridge, Turin discovered a wealth of important materials—*including photographs, films, tape recordings, **and** field notes*—**which** had remained unstudied **and** were badly in need of care **and** protection.

在劍橋大學，圖靈發現了大量的重要資料——包含照片、底片、錄音帶，以及田野筆記——都尚未被研究過，而且急需照料和保護。

which had remained... 是形容詞子句，用來修飾前面所提
及的大量重要資料。

a wealth of 大量的　　　film〔fɪlm〕*n.* 底片；影片
tape recordings 磁帶錄音
field notes 田野筆記；野外記錄

【第六段】

Now, [*through the two organizations **that** he has founded*

*—the Digital Himalaya Project **and** the World Oral Literature*

Project]*—*Turin has started a campaign [*to make such*

documents, found in libraries and stores around the world,

*available **not** just to scholars **but** to* the communities **that** *the*

materials were originally collected from.]

　　現在，藉由兩個他所創立的組織——數位喜馬拉雅計劃跟世界口
語文學計劃——圖靈已經發起一項運動，要讓這些在世界各地圖書館
跟商店發現的文件，能夠讓不只是學者，而且還有原本提供這些材料
的那些社群，都能使用到。

　　found in libraries... 是從形容詞子句 which were found
in... 簡化而來，用來修飾前面所提及的資料。

not just…but… 意同 not only…but (also)…，連接兩個文
法作用相同的單字、片語或子句，在此是連接兩組名詞。
【詳見「文法寶典」p.467】
形容詞子句 that the materials were originally collected
from 修飾先行詞 communities。

found〔faund〕*v.* 建立　　digital〔ˈdɪdʒɪtḷ〕*adj.* 數位的
project〔ˈprɑdʒɛkt〕*n.* 計劃　　start〔stɑrt〕*n.* 發起
campaign〔kæmˈpen〕*n.*（爲…目的的）運動；宣傳活動
available〔əˈveləbḷ〕*adj.* 可獲得的；可利用的
community〔kəˈmjunətɪ〕*n.* 社區；社會；社群
originally〔əˈrɪdʒənḷɪ〕*adv.* 原本

*Thanks to digital technology **and** the widely available Internet,*

Turin notes, the endangered languages can be saved ***and***

reconnected *with speech communities.*
由於數位科技跟無遠弗屆的網路，圖靈說，那些瀕臨消失的語言能夠
被保存下來，而且跟語言社群重新連結起來。

thanks to 由於（= *due to* = *owing to* = *because of*）
widely〔ˈwaɪdlɪ〕*adv.* 廣泛地　　note〔not〕*v.* 特別提到
endangered〔ɪnˈdendʒəd〕*adj.* 瀕臨絕種的
reconnect〔ˌrikəˈnɛkt〕*v.* 重新連結
speech community 語言社群

1. (**B**) 許多學者正在 ＿＿＿＿＿＿ 。

A. 提倡世界語言　　　　　B. <u>拯救快要消失的語言</u>

C. 尋找語言社群　　　　　D. 建立研究語言的組織

make efforts to V. 努力…

promote〔 prə'mot 〕*v.* 提倡

search for 尋找　　***set up*** 建立

2. (**A**) 在第三段中的「那個傳統」指的是什麼？

A. <u>創造語言和文化的紀錄。</u>

B. 撰寫有關語言教學的書。

C. 陳述有關語言使用者的故事。

D. 跟說母語的人一起生活。

refer to 是指　　***native speaker*** 說母語的人

3. (**D**) 圖靈的書是以什麼為基礎？

A. 在印度的文化研究。

B. 在耶魯大學取得的文件。

C. 他在不丹的語言研究。

D. <u>他在尼泊爾的個人經驗。</u>

4. (**C**) 以下何者最適合描述圖靈的工作？

A. 寫作、銷售，及捐贈。

B. 記錄、修復，及獎賞。

C. <u>收集、保護，及重新連結。</u>

D. 設計、實驗，及報告。

donate〔'donet〕*v.* 捐贈　　repair〔rɪ'pɛr〕*v.* 修理

reward〔rɪ'wɔrd〕*v.* 獎賞

experiment〔ɪk'spɛrə,mɛnt〕*v.* 實驗

Test 12

（2014 年大陸北京卷）

Choosing the Right Resolution（決定）

Millions of Americans began 2014 with the same resolution they started 2013 with, the goal of losing weight. However, setting weight loss as a goal is a mistake.

To reach our goal of losing weight—the output, we need to control what we eat—the input（輸入）. That is, we tend to care about the output but not to control the input. This is a bad way to construct goals. The alternative is to focus your resolution on the input. Instead of resolving to lose weight, try an actionable resolution: "I'll stop having dessert at lunch," or "I'll walk every day for 20 minutes." Creating a goal that focuses on a well-specified input will likely be more effective than concentrating on the outcome.

Recently a new theory of incentives（激勵），
including in education, has been discussed. For
example, researcher Roland Fryer wanted to see what
works best in motivating children to do better in
school. In some cases, he gave students incentives
based on input, like reading certain books, while in
others, the incentives were based on output, like
results on exams. His main finding was that
incentives increased achievement when based on
input but had no effect when based on output. Fryer's
conclusion was that the incentives for inputs might
be more effective because students do not know how
to do better on an exam, aside from general rules like
"study harder." Reading certain books, on the other
hand, is a well-set task over which they have much
more control.

As long as you have direct control over your goal,
you have a much higher chance of success. And it's
easier to start again if you fail, because you know
exactly what you need to do.

If you want to cut down on your spending, a good goal would be making morning coffee at home instead of going to a café, for example. This is a well-specified action-based goal for which you can measure your success easily. Spending less money isn't a goal because it's too general. Similarly, if you want to spend more time with your family, don't stop with this general wish. Think about an actionable habit that you could adopt and stick to, like a family movie night every Wednesday.

In the long run, these new goals could become a habit. 【2014 年大陆北京卷】

(   ) 1. The writer thinks that setting weight loss as a goal is a mistake because _____.

    A. it is hard to achieve for most Americans

    B. it is focused too much on the result

    C. it is dependent on too many things

    D. it is based on actionable decisions

( ) 2. In Roland Fryer's research, some students
did better than the others because _____.
A. they obeyed all the general rules
B. they paid more attention to exams
C. they were motivated by their classmates
D. they were rewarded for reading some
books.

( ) 3. According to the writer, which of the
following statements is a good goal?
A. "I'll give up dessert."
B. "I'll study harder."
C. "I'll cut down my expenses."
D. "I'll spend more time with my family."

( ) 4. The writer strongly believes that we should
_____.
A. develop good habits and focus on the
outcome
B. be optimistic about final goals and stick
to them
C. pick specific actions that can be turned
into good habits
D. set ambitious goals that can balance the
input and output

Test 12 詳解

（2014 年大陸北京卷）

【第一段】

Choosing the Right Resolution

Millions of Americans began 2014 *with the same*

resolution they started 2013 with, the goal of losing weight.

選擇正確的新年新希望

數以百萬計的美國人，用跟 2013 年一樣的新希望開始 2014 年，那就是減肥。

> resolution〔͵rɛzə'luʃən〕 *n.* 決心；決定（= *determination*）
> *millions of* 數以百萬的　　*lose weight* 減重

However, setting weight loss *as a goal* is a mistake.
然而，設定減肥當作目標是個錯誤。

【第二段】

To reach our goal of losing weight—the output, we need to control *what* we eat—*the input.*

為了達到我們減肥的目標——成品，我們必須控制我們吃的東西——投入。

複合關係代名詞 what 是兼做先行詞的關係代名詞，在此可代換成 the things that。【詳見「文法寶典」p.156】

output〔'aʊtˏpʊt〕*n.* 成品；成果

input〔'ɪnˏpʊt〕*n.* 投入；投入物

input and output 輸入與產出；投入與成果

That is, we tend to care about the output *but* not to control the input. 也就是說，我們傾向於去在乎成果，但卻不控制投入。

　　that is 也就是說 (= *that is to say*)

　　tend to 易於；傾向於 (= *be inclined to*)

This is a bad way *to construct goals.*
這是一個建立目標很不好的辦法。

The alternative is to focus your resolution *on the input.*
另一個選擇就是將你的決心專注在投入上面。

　　alternative〔ɔl'tɜnətɪv〕*n.* 另一個選擇 (= *another choice*)

　　focus A on B 把 A 專注於 B 上 (= *concentrate on*)

Instead of resolving to lose weight, try an actionable resolution:

"I'll stop having dessert at lunch," *or* "I'll walk *every day for*

20 minutes."

不要只是下定決心要減重，而是要試試一個有行動力的決心：像是
「我午餐要停止吃甜點」，或「我每天要走路二十分鐘」。

> stop 後面加上動名詞表「停止做某事」，stop 後面加上不定
> 詞表「停下來，開始去做某事」。本句意爲「停止吃甜點」，
> stop 後面要加動名詞。【詳見「文法寶典」p.436】

instead of 不…而 (= *rather than*)
resolve to V. 下定決心要… (= *be determined to V.*)
actionable〔'ækʃənbḷ〕*adj.* 具有行動力的
have〔hæv〕*v.* 吃　　dessert〔dɪ'zɝt〕*n.* 甜點

Creating a goal *that focuses on a well-specified input* will
likely be *more* effective *than concentrating on the outcome*.

建立一個專注於特定投入的目標，和專注於成果比起來，可能會更有
效果。

create〔krɪ'et〕*v.* 創造的
well-specified〔'wɛl'spɛsə,faɪd〕*adj.* 明確的
likely〔'laɪklɪ〕*adj.* 可能的
effective〔ə'fɛktɪv〕*adj.* 有效的 (= *useful*)
concentrate on 專注於

【第三段】

Recently a new theory *of incentives, including in education*, has been discussed.

最近一個新的激勵理論，包含教育，已經被討論了。

including in education 可以替換成 education included 或
inclusive of education。

recently〔ˈrisn̩tlɪ〕*adv.* 最近　　theory〔ˈθiərɪ〕*n.* 理論
incentive〔ɪnˈsɛntɪv〕*n.* 激勵（= *motivation* = *stimulus*）；獎勵

For example, researcher Roland Fryer wanted to see ***what***

works best in motivating children to do better in school.
舉例來說，研究人員羅納德・弗賴爾想要看看什麼最能夠激勵學生在
學校表現得更好。

work〔wɜk〕*v.* 有效；起作用
motivate〔ˈmotəˌvet〕*v.* 激勵（= *stimulate*）
do better 表現得更好

In some cases, he gave students incentives *based on input, like*

reading certain books, ***while*** *in others*, the incentives were

based on output, *like results on exams.*
在某些情況下，他給學生的獎勵是根據投入的狀況，例如說讀一些特
定的書籍，然而在其他的情況中，這些獎勵是根據所得到的成果，例
如考試成績。

case〔kes〕*n.* 情況；案例
based on 根據（= *on the basis of*）　　certain〔ˈsɜtn̩〕*adj.* 某些
while〔hwaɪl〕*conj.* 然而　　results〔rɪˈzʌlts〕*n. pl.* 成績

His main finding was ***that*** *incentives increased achievement*
when *based on input* ***but*** *had no effect* ***when*** *based on output.*
他主要的發現是，當這些鼓勵根據投入的狀況時，能夠增加學生的學
習成就，但如果是根據成果來獎勵時，就完全沒有效果。

> when based on input/output 是分詞構句，這種連接詞加上
> 分詞的句型是從屬連接詞 when 之後省略了句意明確的主詞
> 和 be 動詞變化而來。原本的句子是 when they are based
> on input/output。【詳見「文法寶典」p.462】
>
> achievement〔əˈtʃivmənt〕*n.* 達成；成就；成績
> (= *accomplishment*)　　　effect〔ɪˈfɛkt〕*n.* 效果

Fryer's conclusion was ***that*** *the incentives for inputs might be*
more effective ***because*** *students do not know* ***how*** *to do better*
on an exam, aside from general rules like "study harder."
弗賴爾的結論是，在投入上給予的激勵可能會比較有效，因為學生
除了很籠統的原則，像是「更用功讀書」之外，並不知道如何在考試
時考得更好。

> 文章中的 aside from 表「除了…之外（不包含）」，在此等
> 於 except for。但 aside from 在其他地方也能表「除了…之
> 外還有（包含）」，此時就等於 in addition to 跟 besides。
>
> conclusion〔kənˈkluʒən〕*n.* 結論
> general〔ˈdʒɛnərəl〕*adj.* 一般的；籠統的

Reading certain books, *on the other hand*, is a well-set task
over which they have much more control.
另一方面，閱讀某些書是一個他們比較好掌握而明確的任務。

> over which they have much more control 原本的句子是
> They have much more control over reading certain
> books. 因此在形容詞子句裡會有介系詞 over。

on the other hand 相反地；從另一方面來說
well-set〔'wɛl'sɛt〕*adj.* 裝配堅固的；結構牢固的

【第四段】

As long as you have direct control over your goal, you
have a *much* higher chance *of success.*
只要你能直接掌握你的目標，你成功的機會就更高。

> **as long as** 只要

And it's easier to start *again* **if you fail**, **because** you know
exactly **what** you need to do.
而且如果你失敗的話，重新開始會比較容易，因爲你很明確地知道自
己必須做什麼。

> exactly〔ɪg'zæktlɪ〕*adv.* 確切地

【第五段】

If you want to cut down on your spending, a good goal would be making morning coffee *at home* instead of going to a café, *for example*.

如果你想要減少你的開銷，舉例來說，一個好的目標就是早上自己在家泡咖啡，而不是去咖啡廳。

cut down on 減少　　spending〔'spɛndɪŋ〕*n.* 開銷；花費
make coffee 泡咖啡　café〔kə'fe〕*n.* 咖啡廳

This is a well-specified action-based goal *for which* you can measure your success easily.

這是個明確且以行為為基準的目標，以該目標你能輕易衡量你的成功。

for which you can measure your success easily 原本的句子是 You can measure your success easily for this well-specified action-based goal. 因此在形容詞子句裡會有介系詞 for。

action-based *adj.* 基於行為的　　measure〔'mɛʒɚ〕*adj.* 衡量

Spending less money isn't a goal *because* it's too general.

少花點錢不是一個目標，因為它太籠統了。

Similarly, *if you want to spend more time with your family,*

don't stop with this general wish.

同樣地，如果你想要多花一些時間陪你的家人，不要停在這個籠統的希望。

similarly〔'sɪmələlɪ〕 *adv.* 同樣地 (= *likewise*)

with〔wɪθ〕 *prep.* 連同；隨著

Think about an actionable habit *that* you could adopt *and* stick *to, like a family movie night every Wednesday.*

想一個你能夠採用，而且可以堅持下去的具有行動力的習慣，像是每週三的家庭電影夜。

adopt〔ə'dɑpt〕 *v.* 採用　　*stick to* 堅持 (= *hold on to*)

【第六段】

In the long run, these new goals could become a habit.

到最後，這些新的目標可能就會變成習慣。

in the long run 最後

1. (**B**) 作者認為設定減肥當作一個目標是錯誤的，因為 _____。
    A. 對於大部分美國人來說很難達到
    B. 它太過著重於結果
    C. 它需要依賴太多其他事情
    D. 它是根據有行動力的決定

achieve〔ə'tʃiv〕*v.* 達到

dependent〔dɪ'pɛndənt〕*adj.* 依賴的;取決於⋯的

2.(**D**) 在羅納德弗・賴爾的研究當中,有些學生表現得比其他學生好,是因為 _____ 。

A. 他們遵從所有的通則　　B. 他們更專注於考試上

C. 他們被他們的同學激勵

D. 他們因為讀了一些書而被獎勵

pay attention to 注意

3.(**A**) 根據作者的說法,下列敘述何者是個好的目標?

A. 「我要放棄甜點。」　　B. 「我要更用功唸書。」

C. 「我要減少我的花費。」

D. 「我要花更多時間跟我的家人相處。」

give up 放棄　　expense〔ɪk'spɛns〕*n.* 花費

4.(**C**) 作者堅信我們應該 _____ 。

A. 培養良好的習慣並且專注於結果

B. 對於最終的目標樂觀而且堅持下去

C. 選出能夠變成好習慣的特定行為

D. 設定能夠平衡投入跟成果的宏偉的目標

strongly〔'strɔŋlɪ〕*adv.* 強烈地;堅固地

develop〔dɪ'vɛləp〕*v.* 培養

outcome〔'aʊt,kʌm〕*n.* 結果;成果

optimistic〔,ɑptə'mɪstɪk〕*adj.* 樂觀的

pick〔pɪk〕*v.* 挑選　　***turn into*** 變成

ambitious〔æm'bɪʃəs〕*adj.* 胸懷大志的;(目標)宏偉的

balance〔'bæləns〕*v.* 使平衡

Test 13
（2014 年大陸湖北卷）

London's newest skyscraper（摩天大樓）is called the Shard, and it cost about 430 million pounds to build. At a height of almost 310 metres, it is the tallest building in Europe. The Shard has completely changed the appearance of London. However, not everyone thinks that it is a change for the better.

The Shard was designed by the famous Italian architect Renzo Piano. When he began designing the Shard for London, Piano wanted a very tall building that looked like a spire（尖頂）. He wanted the glass surfaces to reflect the sky and the city. The sides of the building aren't regular. So the building has an unusual shape. It looks like a very thin, sharp piece of broken glass. And that is how the building got the name: the Shard. Piano says that the spire shape of the Shard is part of a great London tradition. The shape reminds him of the spires of the churches of London or the tall masts（桅杆）of the ships that were once on the River Thames.

The Shard has 87 floors. At the top, there is an observatory. At the moment the building is empty, but eventually there will be a five-star hotel. There will also be top quality restaurants, apartments and offices.

Before building work began, a lot of people didn't want the Shard though the plans were approved. Now they are still unhappy about the Shard. Some critics say that such a tall skyscraper might be good in a city like New York, but not in London. They say that the best thing about the Shard is its spire shape. But that is the only thing. There is no decoration, only flat surfaces. The Egyptians did that 4,500 years ago. They also think the Shard is too big for London. It destroys the beauty of the city.

Other critics don't like what the Shard seems to represent. They say that the Shard shows how London is becoming more unequal. Only very rich people can afford to buy the expensive private apartments and stay in the hotel. But the people who live near the

Shard are among the poorest in London. So the Shard seems a symbol of the division in society between the very rich and the poor.

The Shard now dominates the London skyline. It is not certain, however, that ordinary London citizens will ever accept it as a valuable addition to the city.

【2014 年大陸湖北卷】

(　) 1. London's newest skyscraper is called the Shard because of _____.
　　A. its cost
　　B. its size
　　C. its shape
　　D. its height

(　) 2. When he designed the Shard, Piano wanted it to _____.
　　A. change London's skyline
　　B. reflect London's traditions
　　C. imitate the Egyptian style
　　D. attract potential visitors

(　　) 3. The critics who refer to social division think
the Shard _____.
A. is only preferred by the rich
B. is intended for wealthy people
C. is far away from the poor area
D. is popular only with Londoners

(　　) 4. Which would be the best title for the
passage?
A. The Shard: Cheers and Claps
B. The Shard: Work of a Great Architect
C. The Shard: New Symbol of London?
D. The Shard: A Change for the Better?

Test 13 詳解

（2014 年大陸湖北卷）

【第一段】

London's newest skyscraper is called the Shard, ***and*** it cost about 430 million pounds *to build． **At a height of almost 310 metres**, it is the tallest building *in Europe*.

倫敦最新的摩天大樓叫作「碎片大廈」，而且它花費了大約四億三千萬英鎊來建造。有著將近三百一十公尺的高度，它是歐洲最高的建築物。

skyscraper〔'skaɪ͵skrepɚ〕*n.* 摩天大樓
shard〔ʃɑrd〕*n.* 碎片
pound〔paʊnd〕*n.* 英鎊；磅

The Shard has *completely* changed the appearance *of London*.

However, not everyone thinks ***that*** it is a change *for the better*.

「碎片大廈」已經完全改變了倫敦的外貌。然而，並非每個人都認為這是一個更好的改變。

completely〔kəm'plitlɪ〕*adv.* 完全地（ = *totally* = *thoroughly* = *wholly* = *entirely* ）
appearance〔ə'pɪrəns〕*n.* 外表；外觀

【第二段】

The Shard was designed *by the famous Italian architect*
Renzo Piano.

「碎片大廈」是由知名的義大利建築師倫佐・皮亞諾所設計。

design〔dɪˈzaɪn〕v. 設計
famous〔ˈfeməs〕adj. 有名的（ = *famed* = *noted* = *renowned*
= *well-known* = *celebrated*）
architect〔ˈɑrkəˌtɛkt〕n. 建築師

When he began designing the Shard for London, Piano wanted
a very tall building *that* looked like a spire. He wanted the
glass surfaces to reflect the sky *and* the city.

當皮亞諾開始爲倫敦設計「碎片大廈」時，他希望有一個看起來像尖
塔一樣的非常高的建築物。他希望玻璃表面能夠反映天空跟城市。

begin 表「開始」，後面接動名詞或不定詞爲其受詞，意義
上無太大差別。【詳見「文法寶典」p.434】

spire〔spaɪr〕n. 尖塔　　surface〔ˈsɝfɪs〕n. 表面
reflect〔rɪˈflɛkt〕v. 反映；反射

The sides *of the building* aren't regular. *So* the building has
an unusual shape.

建築物的幾個面都不是規則的。所以這棟建築物有著不尋常的形狀。

> side〔saɪd〕*n.* 邊；側
> regular〔'rɛgjələ〕*adj.* 有規則的
> unusual〔ʌn'juʒuəl〕*adj.* 不尋常的（= *bizarre* = *odd* = *strange*
> = *weird*）　　shape〔ʃep〕*n.* 形狀

It looks like a very thin, sharp piece of broken glass. ***And*** that is ***how*** the building got the name: the Shard.
它看起來像一片很薄、很銳利的碎玻璃。而這就是這棟大樓如何得到「碎片大廈」這個名字的原因。

> thin〔θɪn〕*adj.* 薄的；細的　　sharp〔ʃɑrp〕*adj.* 銳利的

Piano says ***that*** *the spire shape of the Shard is part of a great London tradition.*
皮亞諾說，「碎片大廈」的尖塔形狀是偉大倫敦傳統的一部分。

> say 加上名詞子句表示說話的內容。【詳見「文法寶典」p.299】
> tradition〔trə'dɪʃən〕*n.* 傳統

The shape reminds him of the spires *of the churches of London* ***or*** the tall masts *of the ships* ***that*** *were once on the River Thames.*

這個形狀使他想起倫敦教堂的尖塔，或是那曾在泰晤士河上的帆船高聳的桅杆。

> *remind sb. of sth.* 提醒某人某事；使某人想起某物
> mast〔mæst〕*n.* 桅杆
> once〔wʌns〕*adv.* 一度；曾經
> *the River Thames* 泰晤士河

【第三段】

The Shard has 87 floors. *At the top*, there is an observatory.

「碎片大廈」有八十七層樓。在頂端，有一座觀景台。

> floor〔flor〕*n.* 樓層
> observatory〔əb'zɜvə,torɪ〕*n.* 觀景台

At the moment the building is empty, *but eventually* there will be a five-star hotel. There will *also* be top quality restaurants, apartments *and* offices.

現在這棟建築物是空蕩蕩的，但它最後會有一間五星級飯店。那裡也會有高級的餐廳、公寓，和辦公室。

> *at the moment* 現在；此時此刻
> eventually〔ɪ'vɛntʃuəlɪ〕*adv.* 最後（ = *finally* = *ultimately*
>   = *one day*）

quality〔'kwɑlətɪ〕*n.* 品質　　apartment〔ə'pɑrtmənt〕*n.* 公寓

【第四段】

Before *building work began*, a lot of people didn't want the Shard ***though*** *the plans were approved*. *Now* they are *still* unhappy about the Shard.

在建築工程開始之前，很多人並不想要有「碎片大廈」，即使這個計畫已經被同意了。現在他們依舊對「碎片大廈」感到不太高興。

approve〔ə'pruv〕*v.* 同意（*= accept = agree*）

Some critics say ***that*** *such a tall skyscraper might be good in a city like New York*, ***but*** *not in London*. They say ***that*** *the best thing about the Shard is its spire shape*. ***But*** that is the only thing.

一些評論家說，如此高的摩天大樓，在紐約這樣的城市應該會很好，但在倫敦並不是。他們說「碎片大廈」最好的地方就是它的尖塔形狀。但那也是唯一適合的部分。

such 可用作形容詞，表「這樣的」，沒有單複數之別，可接任何名詞。【詳見「文法寶典」p.124】

might 可用來表對現在的推測。【詳見「文法寶典」p.317】

critic〔'krɪtɪk〕*n.* 評論家（*= commentator*）

thing〔θɪŋ〕*n.* 正需要的東西；正適合的東西

There is no decoration, *only* flat surfaces. The Egyptians did that *4,500 years ago*. They also think *the Shard is too big for London*. It destroys the beauty *of the city*.

上面沒有裝飾，只有平坦的表面。這樣的建築埃及人四千五百年前就蓋過了。他們也認為「碎片大廈」對倫敦來說太大了。它破壞了這個城市的美麗。

> decoration〔͵dɛkə'reʃən〕*n.* 裝飾（ = *ornaments*
>   = *embellishment*）
> flat〔flæt〕*adj.* 平坦的（ = *smooth*）
> surface〔'sɝfɪs〕*n.* 表面（ = *exterior*）
> Egyptian〔ɪ'dʒɪpʃən〕*n.* 埃及人
> destroy〔dɪ'strɔɪ〕*v.* 破壞（ = *devastate*）

【第五段】

Other critics don't like ***what** the Shard seems to represent*. They say ***that** the Shard shows **how** London is becoming more unequal*.

其他批評家不喜歡碎片大廈似乎要象徵的東西。他們說「碎片大廈」顯示倫敦如何變得愈來愈不平等。

> represent〔͵rɛprɪ'zɛnt〕*v.* 象徵（ = *symbolize* = *be symbolic of*
>   = *speak for* = *stand for*）
> unequal〔ʌn'ikwəl〕*adj.* 不平等的（ = *uneven*）

Only very rich people can afford to buy the expensive private

apartments **and** stay *in the hotel.* **But** the people *who* live near

the Shard are among the poorest *in London.*

只有非常有錢的人，能夠負擔得起購買昂貴的私人公寓和住在飯店裡。
但那些住在「碎片大廈」附近的人，卻是倫敦最貧窮的居民。

> among 表「在…之中」。【詳見「文法寶典」p.552】
>
> the 加上形容詞指「擁有該特質的那群人」，the poorest 指
> 「最窮的人」。
>
> afford〔ə'ford〕v. 負擔得起
>
> private〔'praɪvɪt〕adj. 私人的

So the Shard seems a symbol *of the division in society between*

the very rich **and** *the poor.*

所以「碎片大廈」就好像一個分割社會中非常有錢的人跟貧窮的人的
象徵。

> symbol〔'sɪmbl̩〕n. 象徵
>
> division〔də'vɪʒən〕n. 劃分（= *separation*）

【第六段】

The Shard now dominates the London skyline.

現在「碎片大廈」支配著倫敦的天際線。

dominate〔'dɑməˌnet〕*v.* 支配;控制

skyline〔'skaɪˌlaɪn〕*n.* 天際線

It is not certain, *however*, that ordinary London citizens will

ever accept it as a valuable addition *to the city.*

然而,一般倫敦市民最終是否會認為「碎片大廈」是倫敦的一個有價

值的附加品,現是還無法確定。

ordinary〔'ɔrdṇˌɛrɪ〕*adj.* 一般的;普通的

citizen〔'sɪtəzṇ〕*n.* 市民;公民(*= resident = inhabitant*

  = civilian)

accept A as B 認為 A 是 B

valuable〔'væljəbḷ〕*adj.* 珍貴的(*= valued = worthwhile*)

addition〔ə'dɪʃən〕*n.* 附加(物)

1. (**C**) 倫敦最新的摩天大樓被命名為「碎片大廈」是因為 ＿＿＿＿。

  A. 它的成本　　　　B. 它的大小

  C. 它的形狀　　　　D. 它的高度

2. (**B**) 當倫佐・皮亞諾在設計「碎片大廈」的時候,他希望「碎片

  大廈」能夠 ＿＿＿＿＿。

  A. 改變倫敦的天際線

  B. 反映倫敦的傳統

  C. 模仿埃及的風格

  D. 吸引潛在的觀光客

imitate〔ˈɪməˌtet〕*v.* 模仿

potential〔pəˈtɛnʃəl〕*adj.* 潛在的；可能的

3. (**B**) 那些提到社會階級分化的評論家，認爲「碎片大廈」

_____。

　　A. 只被有錢人喜愛

　　B. 是爲了有錢人而建造的

　　C. 距離貧困的區域很遙遠

　　D. 只受到倫敦人的歡迎

prefer〔prɪˈfɝ〕*v.* 比較喜歡

Londoner〔ˈlʌndənɚ〕*n.* 倫敦人

4. (**D**) 何者是本文最好的標題？

　　A. 碎片大廈：歡呼與掌聲

　　B. 碎片大廈：一個偉大建築師的作品

　　C. 碎片大廈：倫敦的新象徵

　　D. 碎片大廈：一個更好的改變

cheers〔tʃɪrz〕*n. pl.* 歡呼；喝采

clap〔klæp〕*n.* 拍手（的聲音）；掌聲

Test 14
（2014 年大陸山東卷）

The kids in this village wear dirty, ragged clothes. They sleep beside cows and sheep in huts made of sticks and mud. They have no school. Yet they all can chant the English alphabet, and some can make words.

The key to their success: 20 tablet computers（平板電腦）dropped off in their Ethiopian village in February by a U. S. group called One Laptop Per Child.

The goal is to find out whether kids using today's new technology can teach themselves to read in places where no schools or teachers exist. The Massachusetts Institute of Technology researchers analyzing the project data say they're already amazed. "What I think has already happened is that the kids have already learned more than they would have in one year of kindergarten," said Matt Keller, who runs the Ethiopian program.

The fastest learner—and the first to turn on one of the tablets—is 8-year-old Kelbesa Negusse. The device's camera was disabled to save memory, yet within weeks Kelbesa had figured out its workings and made the camera work. He called himself a lion, a marker of accomplishment in Ethiopia.

With his tablet, Kelbesa rearranged the letters HSROE into one of the many English animal names he knows. Then he spelled words on his own. "Seven months ago he didn't know any English. That's unbelievable," said Keller.

The project aims to get kids to a stage called "deep reading," where they can read to learn. It won't be in Amharic, Ethiopia's first language, but in English, which is widely seen as the ticket to higher paying jobs. 【2014年大陸山東卷】

( ) 1. How does the Ethiopia program benefit the kids in the village?
A. It trains teachers for them.
B. It contributes to their self-study.
C. It helps raise their living standards.
D. It provides funds for building school.

(　) 2. What can we infer from Keller's words in
Paragraph 3?
A. They need more time to analyze date.
B. More children are needed for the research.
C. He is confident about the future of the
project.
D. The research should be carried out in
kindergartens.

(　) 3. It amazed Keller that with the tablet Kelbesa
could _____.
A. learn English words quickly
B. draw pictures of animals
C. write letters to researchers
D. make phone calls to his friends

(　) 4. What is the aim of the project?
A. To offer Ethiopians higher paying jobs.
B. To make Amharic widely used in the
world.
C. To help Ethiopian kids read to learn in
English.
D. To assist Ethiopians in learning their first
language.

Test 14 詳解

（2014 年大陸山東卷）

【第一段】

The kids *in this village* wear dirty, ragged clothes.

這個村子裡的孩子都穿著骯髒又破爛的衣服。

in this village 爲介系詞片語，當作形容詞來修飾前面的名
詞 the kids。【詳見「文法寶典」p.545】

village〔'vɪlɪdʒ〕*n.* 村莊
ragged〔'rægɪd〕*adj.* 破爛的；衣衫襤褸的

They sleep *beside cows **and** sheep in huts made of sticks **and** mud.*

他們睡在牛羊旁邊，住在用樹枝和泥巴建成的小屋裡。

sheep 單複數同形，皆不加 s。

beside〔bɪ'saɪd〕*prep.* 在…旁邊（= *at the side of* = *next to*）
hut〔hʌt〕*n.* 小屋　　stick〔stɪk〕*n.* 樹枝
mud〔mʌd〕*n.* 泥巴

They have no school.　*Yet* they all can chant the English
alphabet, *and* some can make words.

他們沒有學校。然而他們全都會唸英文字母，而且有的還會拼字。

chant〔tʃænt〕*v.* 背誦；吟誦
alphabet〔'ælfə,bet〕*n.* 字母表　　　*make words* 拼字；造字

【第二段】

The key *to their success*: 20 tablet computers dropped off *in their Ethiopian village in February by a U. S. group called One Laptop Per Child.*

他們成功的關鍵是：一個叫作「一童一筆電」的美國組織，在二月時送了 20 台平板電腦到他們衣索匹亞的村落。

> key 常見的是意思是「鑰匙」，這裡作「關鍵」(= *answer* = *explanation*) 解。
>
> tablet 常見的是意思是「藥片；石板」，在此作「平板電腦」解，而 laptop 指的是可放在膝上的「筆記型電腦」(= *notebook*)。
>
> ***drop off*** 送到；中途卸貨
> Ethiopian〔͵iθɪˈopɪən〕*adj.* 衣索匹亞的
> per〔pɝ〕*prep.* 每…

【第三段】

The goal is to find out ***whether*** kids using today's new technology can teach themselves to read in places ***where*** no schools ***or*** teachers exist.

目標是想了解孩童能否能藉由使用現在的新科技，在沒有學校或老師的地方，自己學習如何閱讀。

whether 引導名詞子句做 find out 的受詞，whether 與 if
常通用，但 whether 子句做主詞且置於句首時，不可用
if 取代。【詳見「文法寶典」p.484、485】

using today's new technology 為現在分詞片語，做形容
詞用，修飾 kids。【詳見「文法寶典」p.449】

where 為關係副詞，引導形容詞子句，修飾先行詞 places。
【詳見「文法寶典」p.489】

find out 發現；查明

exist〔ɪgˈzɪst〕*v.* 存在（= *subsist*）

The Massachusetts Institute of Technology researchers

analyzing the project data say they're already amazed.
麻省理工學院分析這項計劃資料的研究人員說，他們已經感到相當
驚訝。

analyzing the project data 為分詞片語，放在所修飾的名
詞後，如同形容詞子句一樣。【詳見「文法寶典」p.457】

that 子句做受詞時，that 常省略，原句為 say that they're
already amazed。【詳見「文法寶典」p.479】

analyze〔ˈænḷˌaɪz〕*v.* 分析（= *make analysis*）

project〔ˈprɑdʒɛkt〕*n.* 計劃

data〔ˈdetə〕*n. pl.* 資料

amazed〔əˈmezd〕*adj.* 感到驚訝的（= *surprised* = *astonished*）

"What I think has *already* happened is ***that*** *the kids have*

*already learned more **than** they would have in one year of*

kindergarten," said Matt Keller, ***who*** *runs the Ethiopian*

program.

「我認為所發生的事情是，這些孩子所學的，已經比他們在幼稚園一年學到的還多，」負責衣索比亞計畫的瑪特・凱勒說道。

疑問代名詞 What 引導名詞子句時，該名詞子句要用述敘句的形式，不可用疑問句的形式。【詳見「文法寶典」p.146】
與現在事情相反的假設，主要子句須用過去式助動詞
should、would、could 或 might。【詳見「文法寶典」p.361】
kindergarten〔ˈkɪndɚˌɡɑrtn̩〕*n.* 幼稚園（= *nursery school*）
run〔rʌn〕*v.* 負責（= *control* = *organize*）
program〔ˈproɡræm〕*n.* 計劃

【第四段】

The fastest learner—***and*** the first *to turn on one of the*

tablets—is 8-year-old Kelbesa Negusse.

學得最快的——最先將平板電腦打開的——是八歲的凱爾畢沙・內古西埃。

兩個破折號（——）可以括起重複的、插入語的、同位的，或解釋的用語，本句為同位語的用法。【詳見「文法寶典」p.43】
連接數字與名詞時，使用連字號（-）。【詳見「文法寶典」p.44】

以年齡修飾人名時，放人名前面須使用連字號，並且 year
後不用加 s，反之，人名後面不加連字號，year 須加 s。
例如：Kelbesa Negusse is 8 years old.

turn on 打開（電源）
Kelbesa Negusse〔 kɪl'bisə 'nɛgə‚se〕*n.* 凱爾畢沙‧內古西埃

The device's camera was disabled to save memory, *yet within*

weeks Kelbesa had figured out its workings *and* made the
camera work.
這台裝置的相機被關掉來節省記憶體，但才幾個禮拜，凱爾畢沙就已
經知道它的運作方式，並讓相機恢復運作。

within 可以用於表示「在（時間、距離、區域、能力及權力）範
圍內」，本句中表「在…的時間以內」。【詳見「文法寶典」p.609】

device〔 dɪ'vaɪs 〕*n.* 裝置
disable〔 dɪs'ebl 〕*v.* 關閉（= *turn off* = *shut down*）
memory〔'mɛmərɪ 〕*n.* 記憶容量；記憶裝置
yet〔 jɛt 〕*conj.* 但是；然而
figure out 知道；了解（= *understand* = *work out*）
workings〔'wɝkɪŋz 〕*n. pl.* 運作　　work〔 wɝk 〕*v.* 運作

He called himself a lion, *a marker of accomplishment in Ethiopia.*
他自稱為獅子，而獅子在衣索比亞是成就的標記。

名詞做同位語時，它和前面的名詞是指同一人或事物。
【詳見「文法寶典」p.99】

marker 常見的是意思是「麥克筆；奇異筆」，這裡作「記號」
(= *token* = *symbol*) 解。

accomplishment ﹝ ə'kʌmplɪʃmənt ﹞ *n.* 成就 (= *success*
= *achievement* = *fulfillment*)

【第五段】

With his tablet, Kelbesa rearranged the letters HSROE

into one of the many English animal names he knows.

凱爾畢沙用他的平板電腦重新排列 HSROE 這些字母，成為一個
他所認得的言語英文動物名字之一。

with 可以表示工具或媒介，作「用…；以…」解。【詳見
「文法寶典」p.606】

rearrange ﹝ ˏriə'rendʒ ﹞ *v.* 重新排列 (= *readjust* = *reorganize*)
letter ﹝ 'lɛtɚ ﹞ *n.* 字母

Then he spelled words *on his own.* 然後他就自己會拼字。

then 爲副詞，爲加強其意而放句首時，逗點可以加，也可
不加。【詳見「文法寶典」p.268】

"*Seven months ago* he didn't know any English. That's
unbelievable," said Keller.

「七個月前他完全不懂英文，眞是令人難以置信，」凱勒說。

> unbelievable〔ˌʌnbə'livəbḷ〕*adj.* 令人難以置信的

The project aims to get kids to a stage *called "deep*

*reading," **where** they can read to learn.*

這個計畫的目標是讓孩子進入一個叫作「深度閱讀」的階段，
在這階段孩子能透過閱讀來學習。

> stage 常見的是意思是「舞台」，想這裡作「階段」(＝*phase*
> ＝*step*)解。
>
> get 雖非使役動詞 make/let/have，亦有「使、讓、叫…去
> 做…」之意，但受詞後必須加 to V。
>
> *aim to V.* 目標在於 (＝ *intend to V.* ＝ *try to V.*)

It won't be in Amharic, *Ethiopia's first language*, **but** in

English, ***which** is widely seen as the ticket to higher paying jobs.*

閱讀不是用衣索比亞的母語——阿姆哈拉語，而是用英文，因爲英文
普遍被認爲是較高薪工作的門票。

> *not A but B* 不是 A，而是 B　　***first language*** 母語
> Amharic〔æm'hɑrɪk〕*n.* 阿姆哈拉語
> widely〔'waɪdlɪ〕*adv.* 廣泛地　　***be seen as*** 被認爲是
> ticket〔'tɪkɪt〕*n.* 門票；獲得想望之物的手段；達到目的的途徑
> ***higher paying job*** 高薪工作

1. (**B**) 衣索比亞計畫是如何對村子裡的孩子有所助益？

    A. 它為了他們訓練老師。

    B. <u>它能幫助學生自學。</u>

    C. 它有助於提高他們的生活水準。

    D. 它提供資金來蓋學校。

        contribute to 有助於   raise〔rez〕*v.* 提高

        living standard 生活水準

        funds〔fʌndz〕*n. pl.* 資金（= *money*）

2. (**C**) 我們可以從第三段的凱勒的話中推論出什麼？

    A. 他們需要更多時間來分析資料。

    B. 研究需要更多小孩。

    C. <u>他對這個計畫的未來很有信心。</u>

    D. 這個研究應該在幼稚園內進行。

        carry out 執行（= *execute*）

3. (**A**) 凱勒對於凱爾畢沙可以用平板電腦 _____，感到非常
驚訝。

    A. <u>很快地學會英文字</u>   B. 畫動物圖畫

    C. 寫信給研究人員   D. 打電話給他的朋友

4. (**C**) 這個計畫的目標為何？

    A. 提供較高薪的工作給衣索比亞人。

    B. 讓阿姆哈拉語在世界上被廣泛使用。

    C. <u>幫助衣索比亞小孩能以能用英文閱讀來學習。</u>

    D. 協助衣索比亞人學習他們的母語。

        aim〔em〕*n.* 目標   assist〔ə'sɪst〕*v.* 協助（= *help*）

Test 15
（2014 年大陸江蘇卷）

Most damagingly, anger weakens a person's ability to think clearly and keep control over his behaviour. The angry person loses objectivity in evaluating the emotional significance of the person or situation that arouses his anger.

Not everyone experiences anger in the same way; what angers one person may amuse another. The specific expression of anger also differs from person to person based on biological and cultural forces. In contemporary culture, physical expressions of anger are generally considered too socially harmful to be tolerated. We no longer regard duels（決鬥）as an appropriate expression of anger resulting from one person's awareness of insulting behaviour on the part of another.

Anger can be identified in the brain, where the electrical activity changes. Under most conditions EEG（腦電圖）measures of electrical activity show balanced activity between the right and left prefrontal （額頭前部）areas. Behaviourally this corresponds to the general even-handed disposition（意向）that most of us possess most of the time. But when we are angry, the EEG of the right and left prefrontal areas aren't balanced and, as a result of this, we're likely to react. And our behavioural response to anger is different from our response to other emotions, whether positive or negative.

Most positive emotions are associated with approach behaviour: we move closer to people we like. Most negative emotions, in contrast, are associated with avoidance behaviour: we move away from people and things that we dislike or that make us anxious. But anger is an exception to this pattern. The angrier we are, the more likely we are to move towards the object of our anger. This corresponds to what psychologists refer to as *offensive anger*: the angry person moves closer in order to influence and control the person or situation causing his anger. This approach-and-confront behaviour is accompanied by a leftward prefrontal asymmetry（不對稱）of EEG activity. Interestingly, this asymmetry lessens if the angry person can experience empathy（同感）towards the individual who is bringing forth the angry response. In *defensive anger*, in contrast, the EEG asymmetry is directed to the right and the angry person feels helpless in the face of the anger-inspiring situation.

【2014年大陸江蘇卷】

(　　) 1. The "duels" example in Paragraph 2 proves that the expression of anger _____.
      A. usually has a biological basis
      B. varies among people
      C. is socially and culturally shaped
      D. influences one's thinking and evaluation

(   ) 2. What changes can be found in an angry brain?

    A. Balanced electrical activity can be spotted.

    B. Unbalanced patterns are found in prefrontal areas.

    C. Electrical activity corresponds to one's behaviour.

    D. Electrical activity agrees with one's disposition.

(   ) 3. Which of the following is typical of offensive anger?

    A. Approaching the source of anger.

    B. Trying to control what is disliked.

    C. Moving away from what is disliked.

    D. Feeling helpless in the face of anger.

(   ) 4. What does the last paragraph discuss?

    A. How anger differs from other emotions.

    B. How anger relates to other emotions.

    C. Behavioural causes of anger.

    D. Behavioural patterns of anger.

Test 15 詳解

（2014 年大陸江蘇卷）

【第一段】

Most damagingly, anger weakens a person's ability *to think clearly **and** keep control over his behaviour.*

生氣非常具有破壞性，會減弱我們清晰思考，以及控制行為的能力。

> most 是副詞，作「非常」（= *very*）解，用來修飾
> to think…and…是不定詞片語，用來表示動作，可作名詞、形容詞及副詞，在此為形容詞用法，修飾前面的名詞 ability。【詳見「文法寶典」p.412】
> behaviour 為英式拼法，美式拼法通常 our 會拼成 or（= *behavior*）。

damagingly〔'dæmɪdʒɪŋlɪ〕*adv.* 有破壞性地
weaken〔'wikən〕*v.* 減弱（= *undermine* = *decline*）
keep control over 控制

The angry person loses objectivity *in evaluating the emotional significance of the person **or** situation **that** arouses his anger.*

生氣的人在評估造成他生氣的人或情境的情緒意義時，常有失客觀。

that 是關係代名詞,修飾先行詞 the person or situation,
使用限定用法時,可限縮先行詞的範圍。【詳見「文法寶典」
p.149 及 161】

significance 基本的意思是「重要性」,這裡引申作「意義」
(= *meaning*) 解。

objectivity〔͵ɑbdʒɛk'tɪvətɪ〕 *n.* 客觀性
evaluate〔ɪ'væljuͺet〕 *v.* 評估　　arouse〔ə'rauz〕 *v.* 激起

【第二段】

Not everyone experiences anger *in the same way*; what
angers one person may amuse another.

並非每個人感到生氣的模式都是相同的;某個讓人生氣的事可能
會讓另一個人覺得有趣。

not everyone 爲部分否定,與 all…not 的用法類似,例
如:All that glitters is not gold.【諺】發光的未必都是金子。
what 爲本身兼作先行詞的關係代名詞,稱爲複合關係代
名詞,意思是 the thing which 或 all that。【詳見「文法
寶典」p.156】
分號「;」用來連接沒有連結詞的兩個或多個有密切關係的
獨立子句。【詳見「文法寶典」p.40】

The specific expression *of anger also* differs *from person to*

*person based on biological **and** cultural forces.*
在生物力及文化力的影響下,特定的生氣表達方式也是因人而異。

force 常見的是意思是「力量」，這裡作「影響」(= *influence* = *effect*) 解。

differ from person to person 因人而異；每個人都不同
based on 基於…

In contemporary culture, physical expressions *of anger* are

generally considered *too socially* harmful *to be tolerated.*

在當代文化中，如果用肢體動作來表達生氣的話，一般會認爲會對社會危害甚鉅，而不能容忍姑息。

contemporary〔kən'tɛmpə,rɛrɪ〕*adj.* 當代的
physical〔'fɪzɪkḷ〕*adj.* 身體的
too…to 太…而不能　　tolerate〔'tɑlə,ret〕*v.* 容忍

We *no longer* regard duels as an appropriate expression *of*

anger resulting from one person's awareness of insulting

behaviour on the part of another.

我們不再認爲，當感覺到受另一個人侮辱的行爲時，決鬥可作爲適當的表達的生氣方式。

result from 由…引起，本句使用分詞片語，具有限定作用，相當於關代的限定用法，只能放在其所修飾的名詞之後。
【詳見「文法寶典」p.457】

no longer 不再　　**regard A as B** 認為 A 是 B

appropriate〔ə'proprɪɪt〕*adj.* 適當的

awareness〔ə'wɛrnɪs〕*n.* 知道；察覺到

insulting〔ɪn'sʌltɪŋ〕*adj.* 侮辱人的

on the part of 在…方面；由（某人）做出的（= *as done by*）

【第三段】

Anger can be identified *in the brain,* **where** *the electrical*

activity changes.

　　生氣是可以在腦內被辨認出來的，腦中的電子活動會產生變化。

　　where 引導補述用法的形容詞子句，用以補充說明先行詞

the brain。【詳見「文法寶典」p.162】

identify〔aɪ'dɛntə,faɪ〕*v.* 辨識

electrical〔ɪ'lɛktrɪkl̩〕*adj.* 電的；電子的

Under most conditions EEG measures *of electrical activity*

show balanced activity *between the right* **and** *left prefrontal*

areas.

在大部分腦電圖所測得的電子活動中，皆顯示出左右額頭前部區域中
間的電子活動是平衡的。

measure〔'mɛʒɚ〕*n.* 測量　　balanced〔'bælənst〕*adj.* 平衡的

prefrontal〔pri'frʌntl̩〕*adj.* 額葉前部的；前額的

Behaviourally this corresponds to the general even-handed disposition *that most of us possess most of the time.*

就行為的層面而言，這個發現，與我們大部份的人，多數時間所通常擁有的公平性格傾向是相符的。

> behaviourally〔bɪˈhevjərəlɪ〕*adv.* 在行為上
> ***correspond to*** 符合
> even-handed〔ˈivənˌhændɪd〕*adj.* 公平的；光明正大的
> possess〔pəˈzɛs〕*v.* 擁有　　***most of the time*** 大部份時間
> disposition〔ˌdɪspəˈzɪʃən〕*n.* 性情；傾向（*= character*
> 　*= inclination*）

But when we are angry, the EEG *of the right and left prefrontal areas* aren't balanced *and*, *as a result of this*, we're likely to react.

但是當我們生氣時，腦電圖左右額頭前部區域會失去平衡，因此我們可能就會做出反應。

> when 子句如果出現於句首，必須用逗號與主要子句隔開，因此 angry 後，應該要加逗號，此處缺逗號為原題之錯漏。
> ***as a result of*** 因為　　***be likely to*** 可能
> react〔rɪˈækt〕*v.* 反應

And our behavioural response *to anger* is different from our response *to other emotions*, ***whether*** *positive or negative.*

而我們對生氣的行為反應，與我們對其他不管是正面或負面的情緒反應，是有所不同的。

> whether 為表示讓步的從屬連接詞，作「不管；無論」解，作後面省略了 they are。

> response〔rɪ'spɑns〕*n.* 反應　　***be different from*** 與…不同
> positive〔'pɑzətɪv〕*adj.* 正面的
> negative〔'nɛgətɪv〕*adj.* 負面的

【第四段】

Most positive emotions are associated with approach behaviour: we move *closer* to people *we like*.

大部分的正面情緒都和趨向行為有關：我們會靠近我們所喜歡的人。

> 當關代在子句中為受詞時，關代可以省略，故 people who we like 中的 who 被省略。【詳見「文法寶典」p.154】
> ***be associated with*** 與…有關　　***approach behaviour*** 趨向行為

Most negative emotions, *in contrast*, are associated with avoidance behaviour: *we move away from people **and** things **that** we dislike **or that** make us anxious*.

相對而言，大部分的負面情緒，是與逃避行為有關：我們會離開那些我們不喜歡，或是讓我們感到焦慮不安的人和事物。

> ***in contrast*** 相對而言　　***avoidance behaviour*** 逃避行為
> anxious〔'æŋkʃəs〕*adj.* 焦慮的

But anger is an exception *to this pattern*.

但是生氣卻是這種行為模式的例外。

The angrier we are, the *more* likely we are to move *towards*

the object of our anger.

我們越生氣，就越可能會接近那使我們生氣的事物。

This corresponds to ***what*** *psychologists refer to as offensive*

anger: the angry person moves closer *in order to influence*

and *control the person* ***or*** *situation causing his anger*.

這個狀態與心理學家所說的攻擊型生氣相符合：生氣的人的趨向行
為，是為了要影響和控制造成他生氣的人或是情境。

> ***refer to A as B*** 把 A 稱為 B　　***in order to*** 為了要
> influence〔ˈɪnfluəns〕*v.* 影響　　cause〔kɔz〕*v.* 導致；造成

This approach-and-confront behaviour is accompanied *by a*

leftward prefrontal asymmetry of EEG activity.

這種接近並面對的行為，常與腦電圖活動的左前額不對稱現象一起出
現。

approach〔ə'protʃ〕*n. v.* 接近　　confront〔kən'frʌnt〕*v.* 面對

accompany〔ə'kʌmpənɪ〕*v.* 陪伴

leftward〔'lɛft‚wəd〕*adj.* 向左的；在左的

asymmetry〔e'sɪmɪtrɪ〕*n.* 不對稱

Interestingly, this asymmetry lessens *if the angry person can*

experience empathy towards the individual **who** *is bringing*

forth the angry response.

有趣的是，如果生氣的人對那造成他生氣的人有了同感後，這種不對
稱的情況就會減少。

interestingly〔'ɪntrɪstɪŋlɪ〕*adv.* 有趣的是

lessen〔'lɛsn̩〕*v.* 減少　　empathy〔'ɛmpəθɪ〕*n.* 同感；共鳴

bring forth 造成；帶來

In defensive anger, *in contrast*, the EEG asymmetry is directed

to the right **and** the angry person feels helpless *in the face of*

the anger-inspiring situation.

相對而言，在防衛型生氣的狀況，腦電圖的不對稱會偏向右前額，而
且生氣的人在面對那促使他生氣的情境時，常會感到無助。

defensive〔dɪ'fɛnsɪv〕*adj.* 防衛的

be directed to 對準；指向　　**in the face of** 面對

1.（**C**）在第二段的「決鬥」例子，證明了生氣的表達 ＿＿＿＿＿＿＿。

    A. 通常有其生物基礎　　　　B. 是因人而異

    C. 是受社會和文化所形塑的

    D. 影響人的思考及評斷

       biological〔baɪə'ladʒɪkḷ〕*adj.* 生物的

       vary〔'vɛrɪ〕*v.* 不同　　shape〔ʃep〕*v.* 塑造

       evaluation〔ɪˌvælju'eʃən〕*n.* 評估

2.（**B**）在生氣的大腦中可以發現什麼改變？

    A. 可以看到平衡的電子活動。

    B. 不平衡的模式可以在前額區被發現。

    C. 電子活動與我們的行為是相符的。

    D. 電子活動與我們的傾向是一致的。

       spot〔spat〕*v.* 看到　　pattern〔'pætɚn〕*n.* 模式

       agree with 和…一致

3.（**A**）下列何者是攻擊型生氣的特點？

    A. 接近造成生氣的來源。　　B. 試著控制不喜歡的東西。

    C. 離開不喜歡的東西。　　　D. 面對生氣時感到無助。

       be typical of 是…的特點　　source〔sors〕*n.* 來源

4.（**D**）最後一段討論什麼？

    A. 生氣與其它情緒不同之處。

    B. 生氣與其它情緒的關係。

    C. 對生氣的行為反應。

    D. 生氣的行為模式。

       key〔ki〕*adj.* 重要的　　relate〔rɪ'let〕*v.* 和…有關

       cause〔kɔz〕*n.* 原因

Test 16
（2014 年駒澤大學）

For years, doctors have been saying that to prevent heart disease, patients should pay attention to both the so-called bad cholesterol and the good cholesterol. The good, they said, can counteract the bad. But now, some scientists say, new studies have called into question whether high levels of the good cholesterol are always good, and when they are beneficial, how much.

While some heart experts are not ready to change their treatment, others have concluded that the good cholesterol should play at most a minor role in deciding whether to prescribe cholesterol-lowering drugs. In the meantime, doctors are consulting other experts and asking what to do about patients with high good cholesterol levels. As a result, patients are left with conflicting advice. "There is so much confusion about this that it is unbelievable," said Dr. Steven Nissen, a heart specialist at the Cleveland Clinic.

The good cholesterol hypothesis comes from studies like the Framingham Heart Study, which has followed thousands of people in Framingham, Massachusetts, for decades to see who developed heart disease. The studies showed that if two people had the same levels of the bad cholesterol, but different levels of the good cholesterol, the person with more good cholesterol was less likely to have heart disease.

Researchers learned that the good cholesterol and the bad cholesterol have opposite roles. Both transport cholesterol, a type of fat, but in opposite directions. Bad cholesterol goes to the heart. Good cholesterol goes away from the heart to the liver. So it would seem the picture is clear: "the more good cholesterol, the better." Good cholesterol might even cancel bad cholesterol. Dr. Daniel Rader thinks this idea is too simplistic. He said, "A high amount of good cholesterol is generally a good thing, but it doesn't mean it is so powerful that it creates a total immunity to heart disease." 【2014年駒澤大學】

( ) 1. Patients are at a loss because
   A. doctors are always unwilling to prescribe cholesterol-lowering drugs.
   B. doctors have different opinions about good cholesterol.
   C. doctors always take time in asking patients' opinions.
   D. different researchers give different opinions about doctors.

( ) 2. According to the passage, the correct statement is that
   A. good cholesterol plays a major role in deciding what medicine to give to patients.
   B. bad cholesterol might reduce the levels of good cholesterol.

C. bad cholesterol and good cholesterol
go in different directions in the body.

D. good cholesterol is so powerful that we
can reduce the doctor's advice.

(　) 3. The good cholesterol hypothesis suggests
that one patient is more likely than another

A. to develop heart disease, if one has the
same levels of both good cholesterol
and bad cholesterol as the other.

B. to avoid heart disease, if one has a
higher level of bad cholesterol, but a
lower level of good cholesterol than
the other.

C. to develop heart disease, if one has a
higher level of good cholesterol, but a
lower level of bad cholesterol than the
other.

D. to avoid heart disease, if one has the
same level of bad cholesterol, but a
higher level of good cholesterol than
the other.

(   ) 4. According to Dr. Daniel Rader,

    A. the idea that good cholesterol is strong enough to prevent heart disease is exaggerated.

    B. good cholesterol is strong enough to prevent heart disease.

    C. good cholesterol can prevent heart disease.

    D. good cholesterol enables the body to resist heart disease.

(   ) 5. According to the last paragraph, the best statement is that

    A. good cholesterol is always good enough.

    B. the good cholesterol hypothesis should not be considered too seriously.

    C. all researchers and doctors share the same idea about good cholesterol.

    D. good cholesterol is always bad for you.

Test 16 詳解
（2014 年駒澤大學）

【第一段】

For years, doctors have been saying *that to prevent heart disease, patients should pay attention to both the so-called bad cholesterol **and** the good cholesterol.*

多年來，醫生一直說，要預防心臟病，病人應該注意所謂壞的膽固醇和好的膽固醇。

不定詞 to V. 表「目的」。

prevent〔prɪˈvɛnt〕v. 預防　　***heart disease*** 心臟病
pay attention to 注意（= attend to = pay heed to）
both A and B A 和 B 兩者　　so-called〔ˈsoˌkɔld〕adj. 所謂的
cholesterol〔kəˈlɛstəˌrol〕n. 膽固醇

The good, *they said*, can counteract the bad.
他們說，好的膽固醇可以抵制壞的膽固醇。

The good 是 The good cholesterol 的省略，the bad 一樣是省略了 cholesterol。
they said 為「插入語」，可以放在句首、句中，或句末。
【詳見「文法寶典」p.650】
counteract〔ˌkauntəˈækt〕v. 抵制；妨礙
【counter（反）+ act（效用）】

***But** now*, some scientists say, *new studies have called into*

*question **whether** high levels of the good cholesterol are always*

good, ***and when** they are beneficial, how much.*

但是現在，有些科學家說，新的研究已經質疑了是否大量的好膽固醇
一定是有好處的，以及它們何時是有益的，到什麼程度。

> study 基本的意思是「讀書；用功」，這裡作「研究」
> (= *inquiry* = *a piece of research*) 解。
>
> level 常見的是意思是「水平；程度」，這裡引申作「含量」
> (= *amount*) 解。
>
> how much 字面意思是「有多少」，這裡引申作「到什麼程度」
> (= *to what degree* = *to what extent*)。
>
> when they are beneficial, *how much*
> = when *and how much* they are beneficial
>
> how much 放在句尾，用來強調 beneficial。
>
> ***call into question*** 懷疑；質疑 (= *challenge* = *question*)
> beneficial〔͵bɛnəˋfɪʃəl〕*adj.* 有益的

【第二段】

> ***While** some heart experts are not ready to change their*
>
> *treatment*, others have concluded ***that** the good cholesterol*
>
> *should play at most a minor role in deciding **whether** to*
>
> *prescribe cholesterol-lowering drugs.*

　　雖然一些心臟科專家還沒準備好要改變他們的療法，其他專家已經斷定，在決定是否開降低膽固醇的藥的時候，好的膽固醇的作用充其量也很小。

> treatment 基本的意思是「對待；處理」，這裡作「治療
> （法）」（= *care* = *therapy*）解。
> play a role 基本的意思是「扮演一個角色」，這裡引申作
> 「發揮作用」解。

> *at most* 最多；充其量
> minor〔'maɪnɚ〕*adj.* 次要的；較小的（= *lesser in effect*）
> prescribe〔prɪ'skraɪb〕*v.* 開（藥方）
> *cholesterol-lowering* drugs = drugs that *lower cholesterol*

In the meantime, doctors are consulting other experts *and*

asking *what* to do about patients with high good cholesterol

levels.

同時，醫生正在諮詢其他的專家，並詢問要如何處置有大量好膽固醇的病人。

> what to do about 字面意思是「關於…要做什麼」，
> 引申作「對…該怎麼辦；該怎麼處置…」（= *what to do*
> *with* = *how to deal with* = *how to treat*）。
> *in the meantime* 同時（= *in the meanwhile*）
> consult〔kən'sʌlt〕*v.* 請教；徵求…的意見

As a result, patients are left with conflicting advice.
因此，病人只剩下矛盾的建議。

> leave *sb.* with *sth.* 字面意思是「留給某人某物」，這裡是
> 被動語態 *sb.* be left with *sth.*「某人只剩下某物」。
>
> ***as a result*** 因此 (= *therefore* = *thus* = *in consequence*)
> conflicting〔kənˈflɪktɪŋ〕*adj.* 衝突的；矛盾的

"There is *so* much confusion *about this that* it is unbelievable,"
said Dr. Steven Nissen, *a heart specialist at the Cleveland*
Clinic.
「關於這件事情，有如此多的困惑，以致於這讓人無法相信，」史蒂
芬‧尼森醫生說，他是克里夫蘭診所的心臟專科醫生。

> *so…that*～　如此…以致於～
> confusion〔kənˈfjuʒən〕*n.* 困惑
> Dr. 醫生 (= *Doctor*)【縮寫時要大寫】
> Steven Nissen〔ˈstivən ˈnɪsən〕*n.* 史蒂芬‧尼森
> specialist〔ˈspɛʃəlɪst〕*n.* 專家；專科醫生
> Cleveland〔ˈklivlənd〕*n.* 克里夫蘭【位於美國俄亥俄 (Ohio) 州】
> clinic〔ˈklɪnɪk〕*n.* 診所
> ***Cleveland Clinic*** 克里夫蘭診所【位於美國俄亥俄州克里夫蘭的一
> 　　個多專科的學術醫療中心。被《美國新聞與世界報導》評為美國最頂
> 　　尖的 4 所醫院之一。成立於 1921 年，從 1994 年至 2009 年連續 16 年
> 　　一直是美國排名第一的最大的心血管疾病及心臟外科中心】

【第三段】

The good cholesterol hypothesis comes from studies *like the Framingham Heart Study,* **which** *has followed thousands of people in Framingham, Massachusetts, for decades to see* **who** *developed heart disease.*

好膽固醇假說是來自於像是弗雷明漢心臟研究的研究成果，該研究追蹤了好幾千名麻州弗雷明漢鎮的居民好幾十年，為了要看誰罹患了心臟病。

> follow 基本意思是「跟隨；聽從」，這裡作「追蹤；關注」
> (= *keep informed about*) 解。
>
> develop 常見意思是「發展；開發」，這裡作「罹患（病）」
> (= *fall ill with* = *contract* 〔 kənˈtrækt 〕) 解。
>
> hypothesis 〔 haɪˈpɑθəsɪs 〕 *n.* 假說；假設
> ***thousands of*** 好幾千的
> Framingham 〔ˈfremɪŋhəm 〕 *n.* 弗雷明漢鎮
> 　【鄰近波士頓（Boston）】
> Massachusetts 〔ˌmæsəˈtʃusɪts 〕 *n.* 麻州【位於美國東北部，
> 　首都波士頓（Boston）】
> decade 〔ˈdɛked 〕 *n.* 十年

The studies showed ***that*** **if** *two people had the same levels of the bad cholesterol,* **but** *different levels of the good cholesterol,* the person *with more good cholesterol* was *less* likely to have

heart disease.

那些研究顯示，如果兩個人有一樣多的壞膽固醇，但是有不一樣多的

好膽固醇，有比較多好膽固醇的人比較不容易有心臟病。

> that 引導名詞子句，做爲 showed 的受詞。
> to have heart disease 中，have 這裡作「罹患；遭受」
> (= *suffer from*) 解。
> *be likely to V*. 可能～；容易～

【第四段】

Researchers learned *that the good cholesterol **and** the bad
cholesterol have opposite roles.*

研究人員發現，好的和壞的膽固醇有相反的作用。

> learn 常見的意思是「學習；學會」，這裡作「得知；發現」
> (= *discover* = *find out*) 解。
> role 原本意思是「角色」，這裡作「作用」(= *function*) 解。
> opposite〔ˋɑpəzɪt〕*adj.* 相反的

Both transport cholesterol, *a type of fat*, *but* in opposite

directions.

兩者都會傳送膽固醇，也是一種脂肪，但是是往相反的方向。

a type of fat 為「同位語」，補充說明 cholesterol。

transport〔træns'port〕*v.* 運輸；傳送

in…direction 往…的方向

Good cholesterol goes *away from the heart to the liver.*
好的膽固醇會離開心臟通往肝臟。

> *go away from* 從…離開
> liver〔'lɪvɚ〕*n.* 肝臟

So it would seem *the picture is clear:* "*the more good cholesterol,*
the better."
所以這情況似乎是很清楚的：「好膽固醇越多，就越好。」

> picture 常見的意思是「圖片；照片」，這裡引申作「事態；
> 情況」（ = *situation* = *case*）解。
> 「the + 比較級, the + 比較級」表「越…，越…」。
> 【詳見「文法寶典」p.504】

Good cholesterol might *even* cancel bad cholesterol.
好膽固醇可能甚至能消滅壞膽固醇。

> cancel〔'kænsl̩〕常見的意思是「取消；廢除」，這裡作
> 「消除；消滅」（ = *remove* = *delete*）解。

Dr. Daniel Rader thinks *this idea is too simplistic.*

丹尼爾・雷德醫生認為這想法太過簡化了。

> Daniel Rader〔'dænjəl 'redə〕*n.* 丹尼爾・雷德
>
> simplistic〔sɪm'plɪstɪk〕*adj.* 過份簡化的

He said, "A high amount *of good cholesterol* is *generally* a

good thing, ***but*** it doesn't mean *it is **so** powerful **that** it creates*

a total immunity to heart disease."

他說:「大量的好膽固醇通常是好的,但是這不表示它有強大到足以
產生對抗心臟病絕對的免疫力。」

> ***a high amount of***　大量的 (= *a great amount of*)
>
> generally〔'dʒɛnərəlɪ〕*adv.* 一般地;通常
>
> powerful〔'pauəfəl〕*adj.* 強有力的
>
> total〔'totḷ〕*adj.* 完全的;絕對的
>
> immunity〔ɪ'mjunətɪ〕*n.* 免疫力 < *to/from* >

1. (**B**) 病人感到不知所措,因為
   A. 醫生總是不願意開降低膽固醇的藥。
   B. 醫生對於好膽固醇有不同的意見。
   C. 醫生總是慢慢地詢問病人的意見。
   D. 不同的研究人員對於醫生有不同的意見。

at a loss 困惑；不知所措（= *puzzled*）

unwilling〔ʌn'wɪlɪŋ〕*adj.* 不願意的

take time (*in*) *V-ing* 慢慢地~

2. (**C**) 根據本文，正確的敘述是
   A. 在決定要開什麼藥給病人時，好膽固醇扮演重大的角色。
   B. 壞膽固醇可能會降低好膽固醇的數量。
   C. 壞膽固醇和好膽固醇在身體裡面行進方向不同。
   D. 好膽固醇是如此強大，以致於我們可以降低醫生的建議。

   statement〔'stetmənt〕*n.* 陳述；敘述
   major〔'medʒɚ〕*adj.* 較大的；重要的

3. (**D**) 好膽固醇的假說指出，一個病人比另一個容易
   A. 罹患心臟病，如果和另外一個人有一樣多的好膽固醇和
      壞膽固醇。
   B. 防止心臟病，如果比起另外一個人，有比較多的壞膽固
      醇，但有比較少的好膽固醇。
   C. 罹患心臟病，如果比起另外一個人，有比較多的好膽固
      醇，但有比較少的壞膽固醇。
   D. 防止心臟病，如果比起另外一個人，有一樣多的壞膽固
      醇，但有比較多的好膽固醇。

   suggest〔səg'dʒɛst〕*v.* 顯示；表示

4.（**A**）根據丹尼爾・雷德醫生所說，

    A. <u>好膽固醇強大到足以預防心臟病，這想法是誇大的。</u>

    B. 好膽固醇強大到足以預防心臟病。

    C. 好膽固醇可以預防心臟病。

    D. 好膽固醇讓身體可以抵抗心臟病。

      exaggerated〔 ɪgˋzædʒəˏretɪd 〕*adj.* 誇大的

      resist〔 rɪˋzɪst 〕*v.* 抵抗

5.（**B**）根據最後一段，最好的敘述是

    A. 好膽固醇總是非常好。

    B. <u>好膽固醇假說不該被太認真地看待。</u>

    C. 所有的研究人員和醫生關於好膽固醇有一樣的想法。

    D. 好膽固醇對你總是有壞處的。

      consider〔 kənˋsɪdɚ 〕*v.* 考慮

      seriously〔ˋsɪrɪəslɪ 〕*adv.* 認真地

      share〔 ʃɛr 〕*v.* 共有

【解題秘訣】

此類題目，通常答案都在該段的「最後一句」：

He said, "A high amount of good cholesterol is generally a good thing, but *it doesn't mean it is so powerful that it creates a total immunity to heart disease*."

這不表示它有強大到足以產生對抗心臟病絕對的免疫力。

Test 17

（2014 年上智大學）

Alive — the hibernating man

A man who survived for more than three weeks lost and unconscious on a mountain is believed to have been saved after his body went into a form of hibernation.

Mitsutaka Uchikoshi had enjoyed a barbecue with work colleagues in the popular hiking area of Mount Rokko, an 880m (2,887ft) peak near the port of Kobe in western Japan, when he decided against joining the others for the cable-car ride back, opting to walk down on his own. After losing his way, he slipped, broke a bone and then lost consciousness. The autumn nights were chilly, around 10 $^{\circ}$C, low enough to cause hypothermia or loss of body heat. More than three weeks later he was discovered by a climber. He had almost no pulse and a body temperature of only 22 $^{\circ}$C (72 $^{\circ}$F). After almost two months of medical treatment, Mr. Uchikoshi finally returned home.

Emergency medical teams said that the 35-year-old hiker had survived without food or water after his organs shut down, his pulse slowed and his body temperature fell by a third. They believe that his body functions all but ground to a halt as he lay on the mountainside, a response that saved him. "He fell into a state similar to hibernation and many of his organs slowed, but his brain was protected," Dr. Shinichi Sato, head of the emergency unit that treated the man, said. During hibernation, activity in the body's cells slows to a near standstill, greatly cutting the need for oxygen, and lowering energy consumption. "I believe that his brain capacity has recovered 100 per cent."

Scientists have long speculated that human hibernation is possible, with potential benefits that include enabling astronauts to undertake longer missions in space. It is also hoped that the hibernation process could be used in medicine to slow cell death when treating otherwise fatal conditions such as bleeding in the brain. 【2014 年上智大學】

(　　) 1. Hibernation is a thing some animals do. In
what season do they probably do it?

    A. spring   B. summer

    C. autumn   D. winter

(　　) 2. Who made Mr. Uchikoshi try walking down
the mountain?

    A. family   B. friends

    C. himself   D. work-mates

(　　) 3. Mr. Uchikoshi didn't walk down the mountain
because he

    A. broke a bone.   B. lay down too long.

    C. missed the cable-car.

    D. waited for the climber.

(　　) 4. What causes hypothermia?

    A. cold   B. dryness

    C. heat   D. wet

(　　) 5. After three weeks on the mountain, people
would expect Mr. Uchikoshi to

    A. be thirty.   B. die.

    C. faint.   D. grow thin.

( ) 6. What did Mr. Uchikoshi's body functions do?

    A. They ground on.   B. They raced.

    C. They stopped.   D. They slowed down.

( ) 7. Mr. Uchikoshi did not starve to death because of

    A. the altitude.   B. the mountain.

    C. the temperature.   D. the winter.

( ) 8. Mr. Uchikoshi was treated by

    A. a climber.   B. colleagues.

    C. Dr. Sato.   D. the head.

( ) 9. Because Mr. Uchikoshi's cell activity dropped on the mountain, he needed

    A. extra liquid.   B. less sunshine.

    C. more warmth.   D. no food.

( ) 10. When was Mr. Uchikoshi able to use his head normally again after being rescued?

    A. after several years

    B. immediately

    C. in a couple of months

    D. never

Test 17 詳解

（2014 年上智大學）

【第一段】

Alive — the hibernating man

A man **who** *survived for more than three weeks lost and*

unconscious on a mountain is believed to have been saved

after *his body went into a form of hibernation.*

還活著——這個冬眠的人

　　一個在山上走失、失去意識超過三個禮拜的人存活了下來，他被認為是身體進入冬眠狀態，然後才獲救的人。

who 是關係代名詞，引導形容詞子句，修飾先行詞 man。
【詳見「文法寶典」p.161】

is believed to 為「被動語態」，常用說明客觀的事實，不定詞 to 後面用完成式，可以表示過去式。【詳見「文法寶典」p.377】

alive〔ə'laɪv〕*adj.* 活著的　　hibernate〔'haɪbə,net〕*v.* 冬眠
survive〔sə'vaɪv〕*v.* 存活　　lost〔lɔst〕*adj.* 迷路的
unconscious〔ʌn'kɑnʃəs〕*adj.* 失去意識的
form〔fɔrm〕*n.* 型式
hibernation〔,haɪbə'neʃən〕*n.* 冬眠

【第二段】

Mitsutaka Uchikoshi had enjoyed a barbecue *with work*

colleagues in the popular hiking area of Mount Rokko, an 880m

(2,887ft) peak near the port of Kobe in western Japan, *when he*

decided against joining the others for the cable-car ride back,

opting to walk down on his own.

　　打越三敬當時跟他的工作夥伴們在六甲山──一座 880 公尺（2887 英尺）高，靠近日本西部神戶港的山──的熱門健行地點吃完烤肉後，他決定不跟其他人一起搭纜車回去，而選擇自己走下山。

> had enjoyed 爲過去完成式，表過去的過去；先發生的用過去完成式，後發生的用過去簡單式。【詳見「文法寶典」p.338】
> Mount Rokko 的同位語，要用雙逗點分隔。【詳見「文法寶典」p.39】
> opting to…爲分詞構句，作爲 when he decided 子句的另一對等子句的代替，有補充説明的作用。【詳見「文法寶典」p.459】

Mitsutaka Uchikoshi 打越三敬

barbecue（ˈbɑrbɪˌkju）*n.* 烤肉　　colleague（ˈkɑlig）*n.* 同事

mount（maunt）*n.* …山　　ft（fit）*n.* 英尺（= *feet*）

peak（pik）*n.* 山頂　　port（pɔrt）*n.* 港口

western（ˈwɛstɚn）*adj.* 西部的　　***decide against*** 決定不做

cable-car（ˈkeblˌkɑr）*n.* 纜車　　***ride back*** 回程

opt（ɑpt）*v.* 選擇　　***on*** *one's* ***own*** 獨自

After losing his way, he slipped, broke a bone *and then* lost consciousness.

他迷路之後，滑了一跤，撞斷了一根骨頭，然後就失去意識。

　　slip〔slɪp〕v. 滑倒　　bone〔bon〕n. 骨頭
　　consciousness〔'kɑnʃəsnɪs〕n. 意識

The autumn nights were chilly, *around 10 °C*, low *enough*

*to cause hypothermia **or** loss of body heat*.

秋天的夜晚很冷，大約攝氏 10 度，低到足以導致體溫過低或身體失溫。

　　autumn〔'ɔtəm〕n. 秋天　　chilly〔'tʃɪlɪ〕adj. 寒冷的
　　hypothermia〔,haɪpə'θɝmɪə〕n. 體溫過低
　　body heat 體熱；體溫

More than three weeks later he was discovered *by a climber*.

超過三個禮拜後，他才被一個登山客發現。

　　climber〔'klaɪmɚ〕n. 登山客

He had almost no pulse **and** a body temperature *of only 22 °C* (72 °F).

他幾乎沒有脈搏，體溫只有攝氏 22 度（華氏 72 度）。

　　pulse〔pʌls〕n. 脈搏

After almost two months of medical treatment, Mr. Uchikoshi
finally returned home.

經過兩個月的醫療後,三敬先生終於回到家。

　　medical〔ˈmɛdɪkḷ〕 *adj.* 醫學的
　　treatment〔ˈtritmənt〕 *n.* 治療

【第三段】

Emergency medical teams said that *the 35-year-old hiker*
had survived without food or water after his organs shut down,
his pulse slowed and his body temperature fell by a third.

　　急救醫療小組說,這個 35 歲的健行者器官停止運作後,在沒有
食物及水的狀況下存活下來,他的脈搏速度變慢,體溫下降了三分
之一。

　　by 表「差距」。

　　emergency〔ɪˈmɜdʒənsɪ〕 *n.* 緊急
　　hiker〔ˈhaɪkə〕 *n.* 徒步旅行者;登山客
　　organ〔ˈɔrgən〕 *n.* 器官
　　shut down 停止運作　　slow〔slo〕 *v.* 變慢
　　fall〔fɔl〕 *v.* 下降　　*a third* 三分之一

They believe ***that*** *his body functions all but ground to a halt*

as *he lay on the mountainside, a response* ***that*** *saved him.*

他們相信當他躺在山坡時，他的身體功能幾乎逐漸停止運作，就是這樣的身體反應救了他。

> response 原本意思是「回應」，這裡作「反應」
> (= *reaction*) 解。

> function ('fʌŋkʃən) *n.* 功能
> ***all but*** 幾乎 (= *almost*)
> grind (graɪnd) *v.* 努力；孜孜不倦（做…）
> halt (hɔlt) *n.* 停止
> ***grind to a halt*** 逐漸停止 (= *go slower gradually and then*
> *stop completely*)　　lie (laɪ) *v.* 躺【三態變化為 lie-lay-lain】
> mountainside ('maʊntn̩,saɪd) *n.* 山坡

"He fell into a state similar to hibernation and many of his organs slowed, but his brain was protected," Dr. Shinichi Sato, head of the emergency unit that treated the man, said.
「他進入了一個與冬眠相似的狀態，他很多的器官代謝速度都慢了下來，然而他的頭腦卻受到了保護」，治療這位男子的急診室主任醫師佐藤真一這麼說。

> head 原本意思是「頭」，這裡作「主任」(= *the person in*
> *charge*) 解。
> unit 原本意思是「單位」，這裡作「部門」(= *department*) 解。

the head…爲 Dr. Shinichi Sato 的同位語，要用逗點分隔。

【詳見「文法寶典」p.39】

fall into 掉入；進入　　state〔stet〕*n.* 狀態

similar〔'sɪmələ〕*adj.* 相似的＜*to*＞

protect〔prə'tɛkt〕*v.* 保護　　*Shinichi Sato* 佐藤眞一

emergency unit 急診單位　　treat〔trit〕*v.* 治療

During hibernation, activity in the body's cells slows to a near standstill, greatly cutting the need for oxygen, and lowering energy consumption.

在冬眠期間，身體細胞內的活動會緩慢到幾乎停止的狀態，能大大減少對氧氣的需求，並降低身體能量的消耗。

greatly cutting…, and lowering…爲分詞構句，表示連續、附帶，須用逗點隔開。【詳見「文法寶典」p.457】

cut 原本意思是「剪」，這裡作「減少」（＝*reduce*）解。

activity〔æk'tɪvətɪ〕*n.* 活動　　cell〔sɛl〕*n.* 細胞

standstill〔'stænd,stɪl〕*n.* 靜止

oxygen〔'ɑksədʒən〕*n.* 氧氣

lower〔'loə〕*v.* 降低　　energy〔'ɛnədʒɪ〕*n.* 能量

consumption〔kən'sʌmpʃən〕*n.* 消耗

"I believe that his brain capacity has recovered 100 per cent."

「我相信他腦部功能已經百分之百恢復了。」

that 引導名詞子句，做 believe 的受詞。【詳見「文法寶典」p.24】

brain〔bren〕*n.* 腦　　capacity〔kə'pæsətɪ〕*n.* 能力
recover〔rɪ'kʌvɚ〕*v.* 恢復
per cent 百分比 (= *percent*)

【第四段】

Scientists have *long* speculated ***that*** human hibernation is

possible, with potential benefits ***that*** include enabling astronauts

to undertake longer missions in space.

　　科學家早就推測人類冬眠是可能的，冬眠潛在的好處，包括可以
讓太空人在太空中從事更長時間的任務。

with 表示「具有」之意，相當於 having。【詳見「文法寶典」
p.607】
space 可以指「空間」及「太空」(= *outer space*)，意思是
「太空」時，不加 the。

speculate〔'spɛkjə,let〕*v.* 推測
potential〔pə'tɛnʃəl〕*adj.* 有潛力的；潛在的；可能的
benefit〔'bɛnəfɪt〕*n.* 利益；好處
include〔ɪn'klud〕*v.* 包含
enable〔ɪn'ebl̩〕*v.* 使能夠
astronaut〔'æstrə,nɔt〕*n.* 太空人
undertake〔,ʌndɚ'tek〕*v.* 著手；從事
mission〔'mɪʃən〕*n.* 任務

It is *also* hoped *that* the hibernation process could be used in medicine to slow cell death **when** treating otherwise fatal conditions such as bleeding in the brain.

大家也希望能夠將冬眠的過程運用在減緩細胞死亡的治療中，尤其是治療像是腦部出血的這種沒有運用冬眠技術通常就會致命的情形。

process〔'prɑsεs〕 *n.* 過程

medicine〔'mεdəsn̩〕 *n.* 藥；內科的治療

otherwise〔'ʌðɚˌwaɪz〕 *adv.* 否則；不那樣；不然的話

fatal〔'fetl̩〕 *adj.* 致命的

condition〔kən'dɪʃən〕 *n.* 情況

bleeding〔'blidɪŋ〕 *n.* 流血；出血

1.(**D**) 冬眠是某些動物會做的事。牠們可能在什麼季節冬眠？

　　A. 春天　　　　　　B. 夏天

　　C. 秋天　　　　　　D. 冬天

2.(**C**) 誰讓三敬先生試著走下山？

　　A. 家人　　　　　　B. 朋友

　　C. 他自己　　　　　D. 工作夥伴

　　　mate〔met〕 *n.* 伴侶；夥伴

3.（**A**）三敬先生沒有走下山是因為

　　A. 撞斷骨頭　　　　　　　　B. 躺下太久

　　C. 錯過了纜車　　　　　　　D. 等這個登山客

　　miss〔 mɪs 〕v. 錯過

4.（**A**）什麼會導致失溫？

　　A. 冷　　　　　　　　　　　B. 乾燥

　　C. 熱　　　　　　　　　　　D. 濕氣

　　wet〔 wɛt 〕n. 濕氣

5.（**B**）在山上三個禮拜後，人們會預期三敬先生會

　　A. 口渴。　　　　　　　　　B. 死亡。

　　C. 昏倒。　　　　　　　　　D. 變瘦。

　　faint〔 fent 〕v. 昏倒　　　grow〔 gro 〕v. 變得

6.（**D**）三敬先生的身體做了什麼反應？

　　A. 它們乏味地持續運作。

　　B. 它們加速運作。

　　C. 它們停止了。

　　D. 它們慢了下來。

　　function〔 ˈfʌŋkʃən 〕n. 功能

　　grind on 乏味地持續下去（ = *continue for a long time*
　　　when this is unpleasant ）

　　race〔 res 〕v. 競速；加速

7. (**C**) 三敬先生沒有餓死是因為

    A. 海拔高度。   B. 這座山。

    C. <u>溫度。</u>   D. 冬天。

    starve〔starv〕*v.* 挨餓

    altitude〔'æltə,tjud〕*n.* 海拔；高度

    temperature〔'tɛmpərətʃɚ〕*n.* 溫度

8. (**C**) 三敬先生是由 _____ 治療的。

    A. 一名登山客   B. 同事們

    C. <u>佐藤醫生</u>   D. 首領

    colleague〔'kɑlig〕*n.* 同事   head〔hɛd〕*n.* 首領

9. (**D**) 因為三敬先生的細胞活動力在山上時下降，所以他

    A. 需要額外的液體。   B. 需要更少的陽光。

    C. 需要更多溫暖。   D. <u>不需要食物。</u>

    liquid〔'lɪkwɪd〕*n.* 液體

    sunshine〔'sʌn,ʃaɪn〕*n.* 陽光

    warmth〔wɔrmθ〕*n.* 溫暖

10. (**C**) 三敬先生獲救後，什麼時候能夠正常運用他的腦部？

    A. 幾年後   B. 立刻

    C. <u>幾個月後</u>   D. 永遠沒辦法

    normally〔'nɔrml̩ɪ〕*adv.* 正常地

    rescue〔'rɛskju〕*v.* 拯救

    immediately〔ɪ'midɪɪtlɪ〕*adv.* 立刻

Test 18
（2015 年獨協大學）

"Rare earth elements" are a group of 17 metallic elements that are found in the natural world. Because these elements are used in all sorts of high-tech devices, they are increasingly in demand. In fact, the use of these metals nearly doubled between the years 2000 and 2010.

Despite the name, the quantity of these elements is not so low. Some recent reports have claimed that the amount of rare earth elements may be on the same level as the quantity of copper or lead. Even though the elements exist throughout the world, the quantity in one location is not sufficient for mining profitably. Moreover, these elements are usually mixed with other elements, making it difficult to remove them. This explains why they have been called "rare" earth elements.

Despite ever-growing demands, few countries are mining for these metals on a large scale. One country — China — now handles more than 90% of all mining for rare earth metals. Other countries have not entered this business in part because of the environmental problems that can occur. Extracting the metals creates a lot of waste, including radioactive waste from the uranium, thorium and other elements located in the mining area.

The growing need for rare earth metals may convince some countries to expand their mining. Running out of rare earth metals is not the concern, however. Rather, the question is whether they can be obtained without too high of an economic and environmental cost.

【2015 年獨協大學】

(   ) 1. What would be the best title for this passage?

       A. Environmental Problems of Mining

       B. China's Mining for Rare Earth Metals

       C. High-Tech Devices that Use Rare Metals

       D. The Challenge of Meeting a Growing Demand

(   ) 2. According to the passage, which of the following is true?

       A. The kinds of high-tech devices using rare earth elements have nearly doubled.

       B. Rare earth elements are as easy to remove from the ground as copper or lead.

       C. The actual quantity of rare earth elements throughout the world is not the main problem.

       D. Nearly all rare earth elements exist under the ground of just one country.

Test 18 詳解

（2015 年獨協大學）

【第一段】

"Rare earth elements" are a group *of 17 metallic elements*

that are found in the natural world.

「稀土元素」是在自然界所發現的一群十七種金屬元素。

that 爲「關係代名詞」，引導形容詞子句修飾先行詞
metallic elements。【詳見「文法寶典」p.149】

rare〔rɛr〕*adj.* 罕見的；稀有的　　earth〔ɝθ〕*n.*（化學）土類
element〔ˈɛləmənt〕*n.* 元素　　*rare earth elements* 稀土元素
metallic〔məˈtælɪk〕*adj.* 金屬的　　*natural world* 自然界

Because these elements are used in all sorts of high-tech

devices, they are *increasingly* in demand.
因爲這些元素被用在所有種類的高科技裝置裡，它們的需求量漸增。

device 基本的意思是「器具」，這裡作「裝置」解。

sort〔sɔrt〕*n.* 種類（= *kind*）
tech〔tɛk〕*n.* 科技（= *technology*）
high-tech device 高科技裝置
increasingly〔ɪnˈkrisɪŋlɪ〕*adv.* 漸增地；逐漸地
demand〔dɪˈmænd〕*n.* 需求　　*in demand* 有需要

In fact, the use *of these metals nearly* doubled *between the years 2000 and 2010.*

事實上，這些金屬的使用量在 2000 年和 2010 年之間，將近變成兩倍。

metal〔ˈmɛtl̩〕*n.* 金屬
nearly〔ˈnɪrlɪ〕*adv.* 將近；差不多（= *about*）
double〔ˈdʌbl̩〕*v.* 變成兩倍

【第二段】

Despite the name, the quantity *of these elements* is not so low.

儘管是這個名稱，這些元素的量卻不是這麼少。

despite〔dɪˈspaɪt〕*prep.* 儘管（= *in spite of*）
quantity〔ˈkwɑntətɪ〕*n.* 量；數量　　　low〔lo〕*adj.*（數量）少的

Some recent reports have claimed ***that*** *the amount of rare earth elements may be on the same level as the quantity of copper **or** lead.*

一些最近的報告宣稱，稀土元素的總量，可能像銅或鉛的量一樣，在相同的水平上。

that 引導名詞子句，做 claimed 的受詞。

recent〔'risn̩t〕adj. 最近的　　claim〔klem〕v. 宣稱

amount〔ə'maunt〕n. 數量　　level〔'lɛvl̩〕n. 水平；程度

copper〔'kɑpɚ〕n. 銅　　lead〔lɛd〕n. 鉛

Even though the elements exist throughout the world, the

quantity *in one location* is not sufficient *for mining profitably*.

即使這些元素存在於世界各地，一個地點的量卻不夠有利地開採。

even though 即使 (= *even if*)　　exist〔ɪg'zɪst〕v. 存在

throughout〔θru'aut〕prep. 遍及…；在…各處

location〔lo'keʃən〕n. 地點

sufficient〔sə'fɪʃənt〕adj. 足夠的　　mine〔maɪn〕v. 開採

profitably〔'prɑfɪtəblɪ〕adv. 有利地

Moreover, these elements are *usually* mixed with other

elements, *making it difficult to remove them*.

此外，這些元素通常和其他元素混合在一起，很難移除它們。

moreover〔mor'ovɚ〕adv. 此外　　mix〔mɪks〕v. 混合

remove〔rɪ'muv〕v. 移除；除去

This explains *why they have been called "rare" earth elements*.

這說明了為什麼它們被稱為「稀」土元素。

explain〔ɪk'splen〕v. 解釋；說明

【第三段】

Despite ever-growing demands, few countries are mining

for these metals on a large scale.

儘管需求日益增加，卻很少有國家會大規模地開採這些金屬。

ever- 表「不斷地～」。

grow〔gro〕*v.* 增加　　scale〔skel〕*n.* 規模

on a large scale 大規模地

One country — *China* — *now* handles more than 90% *of all*

mining for rare earth metals.

有一個國家──中國──目前在稀土金屬的全部開採之中，處理了超

過百分之九十。

handle〔'hændḷ〕*v.* 處理

Other countries have not entered this business *in part because*

*of the environmental problems **that** can occur.*

其他國家沒有投入這個事業，部分是因為那樣會產生環境問題。

enter〔'ɛntɚ〕*v.* 進入；開始從事

business〔'bɪznɪs〕*n.* 事業　　***in part*** 部分地（= *partly*）

environmental〔ɪnˌvaɪrən'mɛntḷ〕*adj.* 環境的

occur〔ə'kɝ〕*v.* 發生

Extracting the metals creates a lot of waste, *including*

*radioactive waste from the uranium, thorium **and** other elements*

located in the mining area.

提煉這些金屬會製造許多的廢棄物，包括來自位於開採區域的鈾、釷和其他元素的放射性廢棄物。

> extract〔ɪk'strækt〕*v.* 提煉　　create〔krɪ'et〕*v.* 製造
> waste〔west〕*n.* 廢棄物
> include〔ɪn'klud〕*v.* 包括 (= *contain*)
> radioactive〔ˌredɪo'æktɪv〕*adj.* 放射性的
> uranium〔jʊ'renɪəm〕*n.* 鈾　　thorium〔'θorɪəm〕*n.* 釷

【第四段】

　　The growing need *for rare earth metals* may convince some countries to expand their mining.

　　對稀土金屬日益增加的增長需求可能會說服一些國家擴展他們的開採事業。

> need〔nid〕*n.* 需求　　convince〔kən'vɪns〕*v.* 說服
> expand〔ɪk'spænd〕*v.* 擴大；擴張

Running out of rare earth metals is not the concern, *however*.

然而，用盡稀土金屬並非大家關心的事。

> however「然而」為「轉承語」，用來轉變語氣。
> ***run out of*** 用完；耗盡　　concern〔kən'sɜn〕*n.* 關心的事

Rather, the question is *whether they can be obtained without*

*too high of an economic **and** environmental cost.*
更確切地說，問題在於它們是否能夠不用太高的經濟和環境成本來
取得。

> rather〔ˋræðɚ〕*adv.* 更確切地說　　obtain〔əbˋten〕*v.* 獲得
> economic〔͵ikəˋnɑmɪk〕*adj.* 經濟的　　cost〔kɔst〕*n.* 成本

1. (**D**) 本文的最好的標題是什麼？
   A. 採礦的環境問題
   B. 中國的稀土金屬開採
   C. 使用稀有金屬的高科技裝置
   D. 滿足目前成長的需求的挑戰

   > title〔ˋtaɪtḷ〕*n.* 標題　　challenge〔ˋtʃælɪndʒ〕*n.* 挑戰
   > meet〔mit〕*v.* 滿足

2. (**C**) 根據本文，下列何者正確？
   A. 使用稀土元素的高科技裝置的種類已將近變成兩倍。
   B. 稀土元素像銅或鉛一樣，很容易就能從地表挖出。
   C. 全世界稀土元素的實際數量不是主要的問題。
   D. 將近所有的稀土元素只存在於一個國家的地底下。

   > actual〔ˋæktʃʊəl〕*adj.* 實際的
   > main〔men〕*adj.* 主要的

Test 19
（2015 年早稻田大學）

Logical thinkers make a journey of reasoning from an initial statement (called a *premise*) through one or more steps in a linked chain (forming a series of *premises*) to a final statement (called a *conclusion*). An argument composed of premises and a conclusion is called an *inference*. In a logical argument, all the steps in the sequence are sound. If the initial premise is true, the final conclusion must be true. But in an illogical argument, the steps in the journey do not necessarily follow one after the other. Even if the initial premise is true, the conclusion may be false. Logic is the study of reasoning. It is concerned with sound steps of reasoning, not with whether the premises of an inference are true or false. So the central aim of logic is to understand *validity*.

There are two main types of logical argument. A deductive argument is one in which the premises support the conclusion completely; that is, there are no situations in which the premises are true and the conclusion is not. Inferences of this type are said to be *deductively valid*. An inductive argument is one in which the premises support the conclusion but not completely; that is, there are other possible situations that support the conclusion. Inferences of this type are said to be *inductively valid*.

In the real world, we cannot always find premises that are 100 percent true, so we have to rely on what we can justifiably hold to be correct. 【2015 年早稻田大學】

(　) 1. What can be said about making a deductively valid argument in the real world?

　　A. One has to recognize inferences as valid in all cases.

　　B. One may achieve deductive logic through repeated inductive reasoning.

　　C. One has to show at least one situation in which the initial premise follows from the conclusion.

　　D. One has to survey all relevant situations.

(　　) 2. Which of the following is the correct
understanding of the inference given below?
(Children are always truthful; Taro is a child;
therefore Taro never lies.)

    A. It is perfectly logical because there is nothing
wrong with the reasoning steps taken.

    B. It is perfectly logical because the given
premises are hypothetically possible.

    C. It is illogical because the reasoning steps
taken are not sound.

    D. It is illogical because of the questionable
premise; it is hard to imagine that children
are always truthful.

(　　) 3. Which of the following is the most rational
conclusion about the real world?

    A. We can rely on deductive logic in the real
world.

    B. Professionals such as doctors and lawyers
should rely on deductive logic.

    C. We often have to rely on inductive logic in
the real world.

    D. Logic is rarely useful in the real world.

(　) 4. Which of the following inferences is inductively valid?

　　A. If the burglar had broken in through the window, there would be footprints outside; there are no footprints; so the burglar didn't break in through the window.

　　B. John has nicotine-stained fingers; so John is a smoker.

　　C. John buys two packets of cigarettes a day; so it is John who left footprints outside the window.

　　D. If there are footprints outside, the window is also broken; the window is broken; so there must be footprints outside.

(　) 5. Which of the following is an example of a logical argument?

　　A. All Xs are Y; Z is a Y; therefore Z is an X.

　　B. All Xs are Y; all Ys are Z; therefore all Xs are Z.

　　C. both a and b

　　D. neither a nor b

Test 19 詳解

（2015 年早稻田大學）

【第一段】

Logical thinkers make a journey *of reasoning* *from an initial statement* (*called a premise*) *through one* **or** *more steps in a* linked *chain* (*forming a series of premises*) *to a final statement* (*called a conclusion*).

有邏輯思考的人，做推論的過程，是從一開始的陳述（稱作前提），經過一串相連的一個或是更多的步驟中（形成一系列的前提），達到最後的陳述（稱作結論）。

logical〔ˈlɑdʒɪkḷ〕*adj.* 邏輯上的；符合邏輯的

journey〔ˈdʒɝnɪ〕*n.* 旅行；過程（= *process*）

reasoning〔ˈriznɪŋ〕*n.* 推理；推論

initial〔ɪˈnɪʃəl〕*adj.* 開始的；起初的

statement〔ˈstetmənt〕*n.* 敘述；聲明；陳述

premise〔ˈprɛmɪs〕*n.* 前提

pre ¦ mise	從字根分析，premise 的意思是「先前已送出」，
before ¦ send	說話時，先前的話就是「前提」。也可用：

pro<u>mise</u>（承諾）– pr<u>emise</u>（前提）押韻記憶。

step〔stɛp〕*n.* 步驟

linked〔lɪŋkt〕*adj.* 連接的（= *connected*）

chain〔tʃen〕*n.* 鍊子；一連串　　form〔fɔrm〕*v.* 形成

series〔ˈsɪrɪz〕*n.* 一系列【單複數同形】
a series of 一系列的
conclusion〔kənˈkluʒən〕*n.* 結論

An argument *composed of premises **and** a conclusion* is called

an *inference.*　*In a logical argument*, all the steps *in the sequence*

are sound.

包含前提和一個結論的論證稱作推論。在一個符合邏輯的論證中，該
順序中所有的步驟都是合理的。

sound〔saʊnd〕常見的意思是「聲音」，這裡作形容詞用，
表示「合理的；正確的」。

argument〔ˈɑrgjəmənt〕*n.* 辯論；論證
be composed of 由…組成；包含（ = *consist of* = *comprise* ）
inference〔ˈɪnfərəns〕*n.* 推論；推理
sequence〔ˈsikwəns〕*n.* 連續；順序

If the initial premise is true, the final conclusion must be true.

But in an illogical argument, the steps *in the journey* do *not*

necessarily follow *one after the other.*

如果一開始的前提是正確的，那最後的結論也一定是正確的。不過在
一個不合邏輯的論證中，該過程的步驟不一定依次接續。

illogical〔ɪˈlɑdʒɪk!〕*adj.* 不合邏輯的；沒有條理的

not necessarily 不一定（*= not always*）

one after the other 相繼地；依次地（*= one after another*）

Even if *the initial premise is true*, the conclusion may be false.

Logic is the study *of reasoning*.

即使一開始的前提是正確的，結論也可能是錯誤的。邏輯學是推論的
探討。

even if 即使；雖然（*= even though*）

false〔fɔls〕*adj.* 錯誤的；不正確的

logic〔ˈlɑdʒɪk〕*n.* 邏輯；邏輯學

study〔ˈstʌdɪ〕*n.* 研究；探討

It is concerned with sound steps *of reasoning*, not with

whether *the premises of an inference are true* ***or*** *false*. ***So*** the

central aim *of logic* is to understand *validity*.

邏輯學是有關於推論的正確步驟，不是關於推論的前提是否正確。所
以邏輯學的中心目標是要了解正確性。

be concerned with 和…有關；涉及（*= concern*）

central〔ˈsɛntrəl〕*adj.* 中心的；核心的

aim〔em〕*n.* 目標（*= goal = target = purpose*）

validity〔vəˈlɪdətɪ〕n. 正確（性）；效力
【valid（正確的；有效的）+ ity (n.) = validity】

【第二段】

There are two main types *of logical argument.* A deductive

argument is one *in **which** the premises support the conclusion*

completely; that is, there are no situations *in **which** the premises*

*are true **and** the conclusion is not.* Inferences *of this type* are

said to be *deductively valid.*

邏輯論證主要有兩種。演繹論證是前提完全地支持結論；也就是說，不會有前提為真，而結論不真的情況。這一類型的推論被稱為是演繹上有效的。

in which 為「介系詞 + 關係代名詞」結構，引導形容詞子句，修飾先行詞 one，也可用關係副詞 where。【詳見「文法寶典」p.243】

main〔men〕adj. 主要的（= major = chief = principal）
type〔taɪp〕n. 種類（= kind）
deductive〔dɪˈdʌktɪv〕adj. 演繹的
support〔səˈport〕v. 支持；證明
completely〔kəmˈplitlɪ〕adv. 完全地

that is 也就是說（ = *that is to say* = *in other words* = *namely*）

situation〔ˌsɪtʃʊˈeʃən〕*n.* 情況

An inductive argument is one *in **which** the premises support the conclusion **but** not completely*; *that is*, there are other possible situations ***that** support the conclusion*. Inferences *of this type* are said to be *inductively valid*.

歸納論證是前提支持結論，但並不完全；也就是說，有其他可能的情況支持該結論。這一類型的推論被稱爲是歸納上有效的。

inductive〔ɪnˈdʌktɪv〕*adj.* 歸納的

【第三段】

In the real world, we can*not always* find premises ***that** are 100 percent true, **so** we have to rely on **what** we can justifiably hold to be correct*.

在現實生活中，我們不一定能找到百分之百正確的前提，所以我們必須依靠我們能合理地認爲是正確的事物。

what = the thing(s) that，爲複合關係代名詞。

hold 基本意思是「握著」，這裡作「認為」（ = *consider* = *believe*) 解。

real world 真實世界；現實生活

not always 未必；不一定

percent〔 pəˈsɛnt 〕*n.* 百分之…

rely on 依靠（ = *depend on* = *count on* ）

justifiably〔ˌdʒʌstɪˈfaɪəblɪ 〕*adv.* 正當地；合理地

correct〔 kəˈrɛkt 〕*adj.* 正確的

1. (**A**) 在現實世界中，關於演繹上有效的論證，我們能說些什麼？

　　A. 一個人必須在所有情況中認出有效的推論。

　　B. 一個人能透過反覆歸納的推論完成演繹的邏輯論證。

　　C. 一個人必須至少指出一個情況中，一開始的前提是來自結論。

　　D. 一個人必須通盤考慮所有相關的情況。

　　　　recognize〔ˈrɛkəgˌnaɪz 〕*v.* 認出

　　　　case〔 kes 〕*n.* 情況

　　　　achieve〔 əˈtʃiv 〕*v.* 達成；完成

　　　　repeated〔 rɪˈpitɪd 〕*adj.* 反覆的　　***at least*** 至少

　　　　survey〔 səˈve 〕*v.* 通盤考慮

　　　　relevant〔ˈrɛləvənt 〕*adj.* 有關的

2. (**A**) 下列何者是對以下所給的推論正確的理解？

　　〔小孩總是誠實的；太郎是小孩；因此太郎從不說謊。〕

　　A. 這是完全符合邏輯的，因為採取的推論步驟沒有錯。

B. 這是完全符合邏輯的，因爲已知的前提假設上是可能的。

C. 這是不合邏輯的，因爲推論過程不正確。

D. 這是不合邏輯的，因爲前提有問題；很難想像小孩總是
誠實的。

truthful〔'truθfəl〕*adj.* 說實話的；誠實的
lie〔laɪ〕*v.* 說謊
perfectly〔'pɚfɪktlɪ〕*adv.* 完美地；完全地
given〔'gɪvən〕*adj.* 給予的；已知的
hypothetically〔ˌhaɪpə'θɛtɪkl̩ɪ〕*adv.* 假設上
because of 因爲
questionable〔'kwɛsʃənəbl̩〕*adj.* 有問題的
imagine〔ɪ'mædʒɪn〕*v.* 想像

3. (**C**) 以下何者是關於現實生活最合理的推論？

A. 在現實生活中，我們可以依靠演繹邏輯推論。

B. 專業人員，像是醫生和律師，需要依靠演繹邏輯推論。

C. 在現實生活中，我們常常需要依靠歸納邏輯推論。

D. 在現實生活中，邏輯推論很少是有用的。

rational〔'ræʃənl̩〕*adj.* 合理的
professional〔prə'fɛʃənl̩〕*n.* 專業人士
rarely〔'rɛrlɪ〕*adv.* 罕見地；很少地
useful〔'jusfəl〕*adj.* 有用的

4. (**B**) 以下哪個推論是歸納上有效的？

　　A. 如果竊賊是從窗戶闖入，那外面一定腳印；外面沒有腳
　　　　印；所以竊賊不是從窗戶闖入。

　　B. 約翰的手指沾有尼古丁；所以約翰會抽煙。

　　C. 約翰每天買兩包香煙；所以是約翰在窗外留下了腳印。

　　D. 如果外面有腳印，那窗戶也會是破裂的；窗戶是破裂
　　　　的；所以外面一定有腳印。

　　　　burglar〔ˋbɝglɚ〕n. 竊賊　　　***break in*** 闖入
　　　　footprint〔ˋfʊtˏprɪnt〕n. 足跡；腳印
　　　　nicotine〔ˋnɪkəˏtin〕n. 尼古丁【煙草的成分】
　　　　stain〔sten〕v. 弄髒；沾染
　　　　smoker〔ˋsmokɚ〕n. 吸煙者
　　　　packet〔ˋpækɪt〕n. 小包
　　　　cigarette〔ˋsɪgəˏrɛt〕n. 香菸

5. (**B**) 下列何者是一個符合邏輯論證的例子？

　　A. 所有的 X 是 Y；Z 是 Y；因此 Z 是 X。

　　B. 所有的 X 是 Y；所有的 Y 是 Z；因此所有的 X 是 Z。

　　C. a 和 b 都是。

　　D. a 和 b 都不是。

　　　　neither…nor～　既不是…也不是～

Test 20
【2015 年早稻田大學】

As for the concept of "national character," it is, in the first place, argued that not the people but rather the circumstances under which they live differ from one community to another. We have to deal with differences either in historical background or in current conditions, and these factors are sufficient to account for all differences in behavior without referring to any differences of character in the individuals concerned. Essentially this argument is an appeal to the idea known as Occam's Razor — an assertion that we should not look for explanations that are unnecessarily complex. The argument is that, where observable differences in circumstance exist, we ought to refer to those rather than mere assumed differences in character, which we cannot observe.

The argument may be met in part by quoting experimental data that has shown there are great differences in the way in which Germans and Americans respond to failure in an experimental setting. The Americans treated failure as a challenge to increase effort; the Germans responded to the same failure with discouragement and generally did not continue. But those who argue for the effectiveness of conditions rather than character can still reply that the experimental conditions are not, in fact, the same for both groups; that the stimulus value of any circumstance depends upon how that circumstance stands out against the background of other circumstances in the life of the subject, and that this contract cannot be the same for both groups.

【2015 年早稻田大學】

(　　) 1. According to the text, "national character"
    A. can be divided into numerous important traits.
    B. does not necessarily explain cultural differences.

C. is more prevalent in non-Western cultures.

D. may be useful in promoting group consciousness.

( ) 2. The results of the experiment described in the text suggest that

A. both nationalities performed beyond expectations.

B. neither country achieved notable results.

C. the Americans were always more successful.

D. the Germans tended to give up more readily.

( ) 3. The text implies that experiments

A. are scientific only when conditions do not differ.

B. should only be interpreted in order to provide context.

C. concerning human behavior are meaningless.

D. under the same conditions can get the same results.

Test 20　詳解
(2015 年早稻田大學)

【第一段】

As for the concept of "national character," it is, in the first

place, argued *that not the people **but** rather the circumstances*

*under **which** they live differ from one community to another.*

　　至於「民族性」的這個概念，起初便主張並不是人本身，而是他們所居住的生活環境，使得每個社會都不相同。

> under which 的 which 爲關係代名詞，代替前面的先行詞 circumstances；故介系詞爲 under。而「介系詞 + 關係代名詞 = 關係副詞」，引導形容詞子句。

as for 至於　　concept〔'kɑnsɛpt〕 *n.* 概念；觀念

national〔'næʃənḷ〕 *adj.* 國家的；民族的

character〔'kærɪktɚ〕 *n.* 性格；特色

national character 民族性　　*in the first place* 首先；起初

argue〔'ɑrgjʊ〕 *v.* 表明；主張

not…but rather ~ 不是…而是 ~

circumstance〔'sɝkəm,stæns〕 *n.* 環境；情況【經常搭配介系詞

under，表示「在…情況下」】

community〔kə'mjunətɪ〕 *n.* 社群；社會

differ〔'dɪfɚ〕 *v.* 不同

differ from one…to another 每個…都不同

We have to deal with differences *either in historical background or in current conditions*, **and** these factors are sufficient to account for all differences *in behavior without referring to any differences of character in the individuals concerned.*

我們必須討論在歷史背景或是當今情況中的不同之處，而這些因素便足以說明所有行為上的不同，無須提到任何相關的個人的性格差異。

> ***deal with*** 處理；應付；討論
> historical〔hɪsˈtɔrɪkḷ〕*adj.* 歷史的
> background〔ˈbækˌgraʊnd〕*n.* 背景
> current〔ˈkɝənt〕*adj.* 現在的；目前的
> condition〔kənˈdɪʃən〕*n.* 情況；環境
> factor〔ˈfæktɚ〕*n.* 因素　　suffcient〔səˈfɪʃənt〕*adj.* 足夠的
> ***account for*** 說明　　behavior〔bɪˈhevjɚ〕*n.* 行為
> ***refer to*** 提到　　individual〔ˌɪndəˈvɪdʒʊəl〕*n.* 個人
> concerned〔kənˈsɝnd〕*adj.* 有關的

Essentially this argument is an appeal *to the idea known as Occam's Razor — an assertion **that** we should not look for explanations **that** are unnecessarily complex.*

本質上，這個論點是訴諸於一個被稱為「奧卡姆剃刀」的理論——該主張認為我們不應該追尋多餘複雜的解釋。

essentially〔əˈsɛnʃəlɪ〕 *adv.* 本質上

argument〔ˈɑrgjəmənt〕 *n.* 論點

appeal〔əˈpil〕 *n.* 訴諸＜*to*＞　　　　***be known as*** 被稱爲

Occam's Razor〔ˈɑkəmz ˈrezɚ〕 *n.* 奧卡姆剃刀【拉丁文爲 *lex parsimoniae*，意思是簡約之法則，由 14 世紀邏輯學家、聖方濟各會修士奧卡姆威廉（William of Occam，1287-1347，提出的一個解決問題的法則，他在《箴言書注》2 卷 15 題説「切勿浪費較多東西，去做『用較少的東西，同樣可以做好的事情』。」換一種説法，如果關於同一個問題有許多種理論，每一種都能作出同樣準確的預言，那麼應該挑選其中使用假定最少的。儘管越複雜的方法通常能作出越好的預言，但是在不考慮預言能力的情況下，前提假設越少越好】

assertion〔əˈsɚʃən〕 *n.* 主張

look for 尋找；希望得到

explanation〔ˌɛkspləˈneʃən〕 *n.* 解釋；說明

unnecessarily〔ʌnˈnɛsəˌsɛrəlɪ〕 *adv.* 不必要地；多餘地

complex〔kəmˈplɛks〕 *adj.* 複雜的

The argument is ***that***, ***where*** *observable differences in*

circumstance exist, we ought to refer to those ***rather than*** mere

assumed differences *in character*, ***which*** *we cannot observe.*

　　這個論點就是，我們應該參考那些存在於環境中，可觀察到的差異，而不是我們無法觀察到的，那些僅僅是假設的性格差異。

where〔hwɛr〕 *conj.* 如果（＝ *if*）

observable〔əbˈzɚvəb!〕 *adj.* 看得見的；可觀察到的

exist〔ɪgˈzɪst〕v. 存在 **ought to** 應該（= *should*）

refer to 參考 **rather than** 而不是

mere〔mɪr〕*adj.* 僅僅；只

assumed〔əˈsumd〕*adj.* 假定的；推測的

observe〔əbˈzɝv〕v. 觀察；看見

【第二段】

The argument may be met *in part* *by quoting experimental*

data **that** *has shown there are great differences in the way in* **which**

Germans **and** *Americans respond to failure in an experimental*

setting.

這個論點也許可以藉由引用實驗數據被部分地證實，這些數據顯示德國人和美國人在一個實驗性的設定中，對於失敗的反應有巨大的差異。

meet 的基本意思為「遇見」，可引申為「達到」或「滿足」某標準，在此作論點被「證實」解。

in part 部分地（= *partly*） quote〔kwot〕v. 引用；舉證

experimental〔ɪksˌpɛrəˈmɛntḷ〕*adj.* 實驗性的；實驗用的

data〔ˈdetə〕*n. pl.* 數據；資料 way〔we〕*n.* 方式；樣子

German〔ˈdʒɝmən〕*n.* 德國人

American〔əˈmɛrɪkən〕*n.* 美國人 **respond to** 對⋯做出反應

failure〔ˈfeljɚ〕*n.* 失敗 setting〔ˈsɛtɪŋ〕*n.* 設定；背景

The Americans treated failure *as a challenge to increase effort*;

the Germans responded to the same failure *with discouragement*

and generally did not *continue*.

美國人將失敗當作是一個要更加努力的挑戰；德國人對於同樣失敗的
回應，則是洩氣並普遍地不再繼續。

> **treat** *A* **as** *B*　將 A 視為 B
>
> challenge〔ˈtʃælɪndʒ〕*n.* 挑戰
>
> increase〔ɪnˈkris〕*v.* 增加　　　effort〔ˈɛfət〕*n.* 努力
>
> discouragement〔dɪsˈkɝɪdʒmənt〕*n.* 挫折；洩氣
>
> generally〔ˈdʒɛnərəlɪ〕*adv.* 普遍地；通常

But those *who* argue for the effectiveness of conditions *rather*

than character can *still* reply *that* the experimental conditions

are not, in fact, the same for both groups; *that* the stimulus

value of any circumstance depends upon *how* that circumstance

stands out against the background of other circumstances in

the life of the subject, *and that* this contract cannot be the same

for both groups.

但是那些爲了環境而非性格的有效性，而爭論的人，仍然可以回答說，
那個實驗的情境，事實上，對於兩組人並不是相同的；任何環境的刺
激值都取決於那個情境如何突出並有別於實驗對象的其他生活情境，
而這樣的情況對於兩組人來說不可能是相同的。

argue〔ˈɑrgju〕v. 爭論　　effectiveness〔əˈfɛktɪvnɪs〕n. 有效性

reply〔rɪˈplaɪ〕v. 回答；答辯

stimulus〔ˈstɪmjələs〕n. 刺激（物）；激勵

value〔ˈvælju〕n. 數值　　*depend upon* 取決於

stand out 突出；醒目

against〔əˈgɛnst〕prep. 反對；反抗；以…爲背景；在…的襯托下

subject〔ˈsʌbdʒɪkt〕n. 對象；受試者

contract〔ˈkɑntrækt〕原本的意思爲「契約」，這裡引申作
「情況；條件」（= *conditions*）解。

1. (**B**) 根據本文，「民族性」

A. 可以被分成許多重要的特點。

B. <u>不一定能解釋文化差異。</u>

C. 在非西方的文化中較爲流行。

D. 也許有助於提升團體意識。

be divided into 被分成

numerous〔ˈnjumərəs〕adj. 許多的

trait〔tret〕n. 特點

prevalent〔ˈprɛvələnt〕adj. 流行的；盛行的

promote〔prəˈmot〕v. 提倡；促進

consciousness〔ˈkɑnʃəsnɪs〕n. 意識

2.(**D**) 本文所描述的實驗結果顯示

    A. 兩個民族的表現都超乎預期。

    B. 兩個國家都沒有獲得顯著的成果。

    C. 美國人總是比較成功。

    D. <u>德國人傾向於比較快放棄。</u>

        nationality〔͵næʃənˋælətɪ〕*n.* 國民；國家

        beyond〔bɪˋjɑnd〕*prep.* 超乎

        expectation〔͵ɛkspɛkˋteʃən〕*n.* 預期；期待

        achieve〔əˋtʃiv〕*v.* 獲得　　***give up*** 放棄

        readily〔ˋrɛdɪlɪ〕*adv.* 輕易地

        notable〔ˋnotəbḷ〕*adj.* 顯著的

3.(**A**) 本文暗示，實驗

    A. <u>只有在環境沒有差異時才是科學的。</u>

    B. 只能爲了提供實際情況而解釋。

    C. 有關於人類行爲的都是無意義的。

    D. 在同樣的情況下可以得到相同的結果。

        scientific〔͵saɪənˋtɪfɪk〕*adj.* 科學的

        interpret〔ɪnˋtɝprɪt〕*v.* 解釋

        context〔ˋkɑntɛkst〕*n.* 上下文；背景；環境；情況

【解題秘訣】

最後一題，考暗示的答案通常在該最後一段的「最後一句」：the ***experimental conditions are not***, in fact, ***the same for both groups***…and that ***this contract cannot be the same*** for both groups.

找同義字：conditions do not ***differ*** 就是 conditions ***are not the same***。

全真閱讀測驗詳解

主　　　編／李冠勳

發　行　所／學習出版有限公司　　　☎ (02) 2704-5525

郵　撥　帳　號／05127272 學習出版社帳戶

登　記　證／局版台業 2179 號

印　刷　所／裕強彩色印刷有限公司

台　北　門　市／台北市許昌街 10 號 2F　　☎ (02) 2331-4060

台灣總經銷／紅螞蟻圖書有限公司　　☎ (02) 2795-3656

本公司網址　www.learnbook.com.tw

電子郵件　learnbook@learnbook.com.tw

售價：新台幣二百八十元正

2016 年 1 月 1 日初版

4713269381327